The Special Needs
Parent Handbook

The Special Needs Parent Handbook

Critical Strategies and Practical Advice
to Help You Survive and Thrive

Jonathan Singer

CLINTON+VALLEY PUBLISHING · TENAFLY, NJ

DRIVE4REBECCA.ORG

Clinton+Valley Publishing
Drive For Rebecca, Inc.
Tenafly, NJ
Drive4Rebecca.org

2nd ed.

ISBN: 978-1-4700-4721-4

Printed in the United States of America
This book is printed on acid-free paper.

DEDICATION

The Special Needs **Parent Handbook** is dedicated with gratitude to the interim Superintendent (at the time of writing) and to other officials in our school district, without whose inflexibility on a very minor issue this book might never have been finished.

Their actions enabled me to learn firsthand how to assert my rights, and inspired me to complete the chapter on advocacy and finish this long work in progress. To settle our disagreement they gave us $500 which we donated to launch **Advocacy For All,** a new initiative to help parents advocate more effectively on behalf of their children. I am eternally grateful for their stubbornness.

If you find yourself in a situation that puts you at odds with your school system, let my experience inspire you to be strong and take action after you have explored every reasonable way to work things out.

ACKNOWLEDGEMENTS

Several years ago, on a Yahoo discussion group, I began answering questions posed by other families who needed information to help their children who had the same genetic disorder as my daughter Rebecca has.

I started saving my answers and decided that one day I would write a book and share some of the things I had learned over the years. Subsequently I wrote a few chapters and posted them on our Drive4Rebecca.org web site, and they have been downloaded by tens of thousands of people.

I really got going on the book at the end of 2008 when faced with a dispute with our local school district over a minor issue. Several more chapters were finished at that point, but it was the experience of challenging the school district that inspired me to finish the book and start the Advocacy For All initiative. I wanted to share what I had learned to help other families.

This book was made possible in large part by the kindness of many people who helped Rebecca enjoy things that most people take for granted, such as participating in Girl Scouts or spending time in places like Starbucks.

Thanks to everyone who read through my many drafts and provided valuable and insightful input, including Bill Bishop, Rick Colosimo, Colleen O'Donnell, David Halper, Shelley Millstein, Greg Pitkoff, Mark Shanock, David Singer, Michey Singer, Ross Slater and especially Ron Drenger for his terrific editing.

Thank you to Alan Bower and AuthorHouse. A special thanks to Sharon Schanzer and Sara Seagull of Red Letter Day Graphic Design for donating a substantial amount of time and energy to produce the wonderful cover design, formatting, and for helping see this project through to its completion.

I want to thank Rebecca, my angel, for teaching me so many things over the years, for being such a good sport while I dragged her to many places she probably didn't want to go to but had no way of telling me, and for being the true inspiration for this book. I want to thank my son Sam for always providing comic relief and the right balance in our household by being so easy and such a delight despite all of the challenges we have faced over the years. Finally, I want to thank my wife, Michey, for all of her helpful input on the book; for her faith in me; for her patience, encouragement, love and support; for being the rock I can always lean on, and for her strength in keeping everything together for our family.

Special Needs Parents Zone

To Our Readers:

To expand upon the topics covered in The Special Needs Parent Handbook, we have created **The Special Needs Parent Zone**™.

Please join our online discussion group to share information and strategies that have worked for you, and to learn from other families, so we can all help one another to survive and thrive in caring for our children with special needs.

Learn more at **Drive4Rebecca.org**

Jon Singer

Drive For Rebecca, Inc.
Tenafly, New Jersey
info@Drive4Rebecca.org

CONTENTS

INTRODUCTION

THERE IS LIGHT AT THE END OF THE TUNNEL
But it's a long tunnel

Do you have a child with special needs? My wife Michey and I do, too, and it's exhausting, overwhelming and impossible at times. Over the years, with lots of trial and error, we have learned a great deal about what works and what doesn't work so well in caring for our daughter, Rebecca. We have written this book to share our life lessons on how to make the most of a very challenging situation and how to avoid some of the pitfalls, and to help you enjoy your life to the fullest with your family.

The top five reasons to read this book (or to give it to a friend or relative who has a child with special needs):

1 To gain strategies on how to make your life more enjoyable and manageable and how to make it through some of the most difficult times. There is typically light at the end of the tunnel and things eventually do get better, no matter how bleak they look at the moment.

2 To learn how to find the best childcare so you can get a break and focus on relationships with your significant other, with family and with friends.

3 To guide you on including your child in many activities in your community, with typically developing children, and in everything you do.

4 **To help you advocate more effectively and fight for the rights of your child.** While the people making educational decisions about your child may have the best intentions, they have a huge conflict of interest and are ultimately guided by policies that do not put your child's best interests first. They work for the school district and must minimize public expenditures — and that can come at the expense of your child's future.

5 **100% of the proceeds from the sale of this book will help fund Advocacy for All,** a new initiative to provide families with free assistance with advocacy. Parents of children with special needs must know their rights so they can pursue the best possible educational options for their children, with the least amount of stress.

BE PREPARED FOR THE CHALLENGES
Don't be scared, get prepared

Our daughter, who is now fourteen years old, is severely affected by a rare genetic disorder called Phelan-McDermid Syndrome that causes autistic tendencies, and we have dealt with a lot challenges over the years. She needs constant one-on-one attention and will likely need that level of care for the rest of her life. Do my wife and I argue? Of course we do. Do we have rough days and nights when we are completely exhausted and feel miserable? Absolutely. Could our relationship have stayed this strong, and would we have had the strength to face the ongoing challenges, without using strategies that you will find in the following pages? Not a chance.

In a terrific book called "Protecting the Gift," which is all about keeping your family from harm, Gavin De Becker writes, "don't be scared, be prepared." That's what this book is all about, preparing yourself for the many challenges you face in life so you can attain the best possible results at the lowest financial and emotional cost.

SAY HELLO TO HOLLAND
And ciao to Italy

To explain how it feels to have a child with special needs, Emily Perl Kingsley wrote a story as if she was planning a dream trip to Italy. She has been thinking about the trip for her entire life, making all sorts of arrangements, and has great expectations about the amazing foods, the wine, the beautiful countryside, and all the special things to enjoy when she arrives.

When she gets off the plane, however, she is surprised to find herself in Holland. She realizes she won't have the great Italian food and wines she looked forward to, and she can't visit the Sistine Chapel or the Amalfi Coast. In fact, she finds out she will never go to Italy and she is stuck in Holland for the rest of her life. At first she is very upset with the news. But once she starts looking around, she realizes Holland has many beautiful things to enjoy and appreciate — just different things than what Italy has to offer. She goes on to write that the pain will be there forever but if you spend your life thinking about all of the things you will miss you will never be able to appreciate all the wonderful things about what you have. (To read the essay, search for "Welcome to Holland" in Google.com.)

Well, that's one way to look at it. And yes, I am sure Holland is lovely. But I really, really, really wanted to go to Italy and can't help but think about it. Don't get me wrong. While I love my daughter Rebecca more than practically anything in the world, life as the parent of a child with special needs can really be a bummer, especially when you first get your child's diagnosis. It can take a long time to get used to it — and you never get completely used to it.

It can be hard for parents to find beauty in very challenging situations, especially with children whose behavior or health gets worse with each passing day. A friend whose child died a slow and tragic death put it best when he said he misses his daughter badly, but doesn't miss all the problems and the terrible sadness.

LIFE CAN BE REALLY DIFFICULT
It is never easy

The difficulties that arise from having a child with special needs can be overwhelming, exhausting and all-consuming. It's like caring for a parent with Alzheimer's, except it starts at birth and may never end. It is very hard for anyone who is not in a similar situation to really understand how traumatic, life-changing, stressful and devastating it can be, and the catastrophic impact it can have on a family. It can also be a financial disaster, on top of everything else.

So the situation we are in is incredibly difficult, no matter how you look at it. Let's just get that off of our chests. Take a deep breath in...then breathe out. Ahhhh, doesn't that feel better? No, I didn't think so, but it is what it is.

Kids with special needs can have very complicated issues, and sometimes there are no simple answers. We once brought our daughter to the emergency room with a limp and a mysterious rash on her leg. She was in the hospital for nearly a week as the doctors struggled to make sense of her symptoms. An ultrasound identified a kidney problem that had nothing to do with the limp and that required surgery, but that did not explain the rash. The doctors could not figure out a connection. Finally, it was discovered that it was just a simple case of strep throat that had caused our daughter's limp and skin condition. Dealing with the confusion was extremely frustrating and then we had to deal with the problem we found requiring surgery, but that's another story. Unfortunately, these sorts of situations are all too commonplace for many families who have children with special needs.

Does any of this change the way I feel about my sweet angel of a daughter? Not at all; she is amazing. I love her very much, love spending time with her, and do my best to include her in nearly everything we do as a family. I have often joked that one of the reasons I love her so much is that when I come home from work and the dog is barking, my son is yelling, and my wife is asking me to take out the trash, Rebecca just walks up to me and gives me a big hug. How could you not love that?

LIFE CAN BE GOOD
There is a lot to enjoy

So welcome to Holland. You will face numerous challenges, but there are so many things to enjoy as long as you don't get too bogged down focusing on the negatives. I once read that there's not much point in worrying about bad things happening — they happen automatically so why spend time worrying about them? Instead, celebrate life whenever possible and do what you can to be prepared to deal with problems as they occur.

This handbook is designed to help you handle the constant challenges of caring for an individual with special needs, and to enable you to focus on what is most important in your life. The following chapters are a compilation of life lessons and other information to help you effectively negotiate the maze of financial, educational and emotional decisions that we face day to day and over long run as caregivers to children with special needs.

The book discusses many strategies you can employ to make life somewhat easier for you and to provide greater opportunities to your child. Do not feel pressured to do everything at once. Set small goals to get yourself started. Keep at it and you will gain the confidence to continue moving ahead. While you will need to work hard at it, because it is never easy, you and your family can grow stronger physically, mentally, emotionally and spiritually, and you can make the most of your situation to enjoy life more fully.

ADVOCACY FOR ALL™
So every child can be their best™

All proceeds from sales of *The Special Needs* **Parent Handbook** will support Advocacy for All, a new initiative of The Drive For Rebecca (www.Drive4Rebecca.org) to help families advocate more effectively on behalf of their children with special needs. The Drive For Rebecca is a foundation we created several years ago to raise funds for advocacy, research, education and to increase awareness of autism.

When parents of children with special needs do not know their rights, or are unable to be strong advocates, the children can become victims of a form of unintentional child abuse by the school system. Without a powerful voice to represent them and advocate on their behalf, they may be denied the best possible education and will be unable to reach their potential.

Consider the family for which English is a second language, or with a single mom, or with two working parents who work so hard they barely get to see their kids. These families are often at a tremendous disadvantage because of a lack of understanding of the law, an inability to communicate, or, in the case of many single moms, the sheer exhaustion of just trying to keep one's head above water in order to survive each day.

Through Advocacy for All, The Drive for Rebecca will help generate funds to support not-for-profit organizations that provide free advocacy services to families that have children with special needs. We aim to offer free assistance to anyone in need so that every child can be their best.

Please join us and support our effort to help make sure these kids don't get left behind.

SUMMARY

Life with a child with special needs can be filled with endless joys and constant challenges.

Learn from mistakes we made and minimize the difficulties.

Take the time to enjoy life with your family to the fullest.

1
KEEPING
THE FAMILY
TOGETHER

OVERVIEW

It is vital to the survival of your relationship with your significant other to make time for yourselves.

Spending quality time with all of your children is important.

Celebrate even the smallest bit of progress made each day by your child with special needs and by everyone in your family.

YOU AND YOUR SIGNIFICANT OTHER
Spending time together is critical

For me and Michey, keeping the family together (and as happy as possible) is the number one goal. We aim to have the best relationship with each other, with our typically developing son, and with our daughter Rebecca who has special needs.

Having a child with special needs is a constant, always-changing series of challenges — emotional, financial and physical — and the stress can easily overwhelm even the strongest and most positive individuals.

There are a number of strategies you can employ to cope with the neverending roller coaster ride, which can help preserve and strengthen your relationship, and keep your life in balance.

One of the most important things for our relationship was to make sure we made time to be together and time for ourselves individually. We have had babysitters almost every Wednesday and Saturday night since Rebecca was born, allowing us to get a break and do something nice as a couple or with friends. We also take time individually to be with our friends and pursue our interests. My wife participates in a book club, goes to yoga and knits. I exercise on a regular basis and spend time with friends seeing movies or going out to dinner. Babysitting is not an option for everyone, but don't overlook resources that may help you get the breaks you need. Respite programs have helped defray some of the enormous costs of caring for our daughter, and family and friends have often been there to help as well. We are fortunate that we have family living nearby. They have been a tremendous help in allowing us to take vacations or to get some down time.

When we don't have the time or budget for full vacations, we try to plan short weekend or overnight getaways, sometimes at the homes of friends or family members to keep the cost down. We periodically arrange to spend a day together locally; I take off from work, and between babysitting and school the kids are taken care of all day. It is a good way for us to reconnect and have a minivacation together — maybe spending the day walking around New York City, or doing something nice together close to home.

To give my wife a break, I often take one or both kids to their grandparent's house which is about an hour away from our home. The kids really enjoy seeing their grandparents, and vice versa, and Michey gets several hours to do whatever she wants without any of us around to disturb her.

Good communication has also been key for us. While things have not always gone completely smoothly, we have been able to build on and strengthen our relationship by working together as a team. When we butt heads on an issue, it usually comes down to a difference in style. I like to jump out of bed first thing in the morning, generally have lots of energy, and am ready to hit the deck running. I also happen to be a bit messy in the way that I do things. My wife, on the other hand, is practically unable to speak when she first wakes up, especially until she has had a cup of coffee. She is very neat and organized. After hearing about our mornings, which had been a source of a little contention, someone made the suggestion that I get the morning routine started, bring a cup of coffee to my wife in bed, and begin getting the kids ready. Then she could finish things up, get the kids dressed and ready for school, and clean up the messes I made. This strategy really made a difference for us.

TIME WITH THE KIDS
Make the time to have quality time

We try to schedule activities together as a family and spend time individually with each of our children. We want to make sure that our son, Sam, who is a typically developing child, knows that he can have our undivided attention, and have special time with us, even if Rebecca gets so much of our attention — and attention from babysitters and therapists — on a regular basis.

I plan activities with each of our kids individually and together with the two of them, including overnight trips, going to the zoo, or just taking a walk around town. We get to spend some nice time together and my wife gets some well deserved time alone and peace and quiet (every so often she gives me a break too!).

BRING A FRIEND
Keep a sibling happy — welcome friends

Our home has been filled with various caregivers and therapists over the years with a big focus on Rebecca. Because Sam and Rebecca don't play together, we have found it very helpful — for him and for our own sanity — to open our home to his friends. Sam often invites friends for dinner, and on weekends or school breaks his friends sometimes sleep over (generally one or two at a time, at most), and sometimes they join us on outings to New York City, the zoo, or wherever we go as a family.

Sam's friends have gotten to know Rebecca and have been very nice to her as a result of all of the time they have spent in our home and with our family. When we all venture out somewhere together, and Rebecca needs extra attention (for example, if Rebecca is unable to sit quietly while we are having lunch), my wife or I can help Rebecca while the other one stays with Sam and his friend.

One time I took Rebecca, Sam, and my nephew Jeremy to a free kids concert at Lincoln Center through its special program for children with disabilities. Toward the end of the show Rebecca was starting to get antsy. I took her out of the theater so she wouldn't disturb anyone, and Sam was able to enjoy the rest of the concert with his big cousin Jeremy. When Sam has someone along to keep him occupied, Rebecca's issues are less of a burden on him and he can get more enjoyment out of the activity. If it can work within our budget, we would even like to figure out a way to bring one of Sam's friends along with us on future vacations.

Being proactive and including Sam's friends in family activities has also had a very positive unintended consequence. Sam has more frequent sleepovers at his friends' homes and is sometimes invited to join his friends and their families in nice activities, which can make things easier for us (our home gets very quiet when Sam isn't around).

Michey and I had originally planned to have a third child, but we stopped short after two because we thought it would be too much for us to handle. Someone once told me that two is good, but with three or more you are outnumbered. Inviting friends to join us for family activities is the next best thing to our kids having another sibling, and we won't have to pay another college tuition.

YOUR FAMILY CIRCLE
Sharing the love and hard work

Dealing with all of the complex issues we face with our children takes teamwork, and your team includes anyone you can recruit who wants to help. If you build a "family circle" of friends and family members, the responsibility of caring for your child can be shared, and that benefits everyone in so many ways.

Try to meet or speak with all the people you have identified who may be willing to help, and explain some of your most difficult challenges to them. Because our family has taken on some important responsibilities, my wife and I have been able to enjoy a good deal of free time together and have received help with our kids many times when we needed it the most. Because Michey's mom has stayed over at our home a number of times together with a babysitter to watch the kids we have have been able to get away and have some nice breaks.

We are very close to my brother's family, in our relationship and geographically (they live only a few minutes away). Sam spends a good deal of time with them and, since Rebecca is not a typical big sister and doesn't know how to play, his cousins are more like older siblings. That's really important to him and to our family. Our nieces are also like big sisters to Rebecca and have started baby-sitting, which has been a big help.

One thing that is very important in our relationships with our "family circle," is that we help one another by bartering. This is especially true with my brother and his wife. There have been times when we have watched their kids so they could take vacations alone together, and my wife used to take their kids shopping when they were young since my sister-in-law found it frustrating trying to buy clothing for our nieces. Your goal should be to make your "family circle" relationships mutually beneficial.

The main point, which you already know, is that caring for a child with special needs is a difficult, challenging and lifelong task. On the other hand, as a friend of mine so aptly said, caring for a child with special needs can bring blessings to all who help along the way — and your closest friends and family can help you in all areas of life. You need to take the time to explain this to everyone and to find out where each individual thinks that he or she can contribute. If you ask, people will help. They will feel a great sense of pride by playing such an important role in your life and will find their lives enriched by the experience.

You may not always be there for your child if you become ill or disabled or when you are gone (or if you have run off to an unknown location in Mexico). The most important people in your life, and the guardians of your children, as specified in your will, should know there are other people who can help. That way they will not be overwhelmed by the thought of how they would handle things if you and your significant other were no longer around.

OTHER PEOPLE HAVE IMPORTANT ISSUES
Don't alienate friends by minimizing their issues

Consider the following when speaking with other people about your issues or when they are telling you about a challenge they are experiencing with their typically developing child.

While it may be easy to dismiss issues that other people are facing as comparatively unimportant ("my child does not listen" or "I do not know what to do with my wild two-year-old"), do not make the mistake of minimizing what they perceive as major problems in their lives.

I recall a friend telling me about something that was going on with his daughter.

11

He said, "I guess I shouldn't complain because it's nothing compared to what you have to deal with in your life." I said his issues were just as important to him as mine were to me, and I all of a sudden came to the realization that if I started thinking that other people's problems paled in comparison to my own, I would probably lose all of my friends. We all need our friends to survive, and we must keep our relationships with them strong — especially those of us who have children with special needs, since our time with friends may be limited because of our hectic lives.

We all have issues to deal with in life, and we are all entitled to deem anything we want as important. For parents of children with special needs, just because we may feel that many of our experiences are far more difficult to contend with than what other people have on their plates, it does not give us carte blanche to dismiss or negate the feelings of others.

SOMEONE HAS A MORE DIFFICULT SITUATION THAN YOURS
There are other people who are far worse off than you

While it doesn't work for everyone, try to keep in mind that there is always someone whose situation is far worse than yours, and everything is relative. When I spent the night in the hospital with Rebecca after she had her tonsils removed, she was able to sleep peacefully through the night. I was up all night, however, listening to the mother who was trying to comfort her fourteen-year-old daughter (who had the body of a four-year-old) in the next bed. This young girl was on a respirator, had a feeding tube, and needed to be turned every thirty minutes. She was up all night and seemed to be in agony, constantly calling her mother's name for help. Compared to what her parents must deal with every day, caring for Rebecca is a breeze.

Then there was the mother I knew who had a child with autism and whose husband died on 9/11 in the World Trade Center. Think about the many families with twins or triplets with special needs, and finally, imagine someone in a country in the developing world dealing with a situation like ours, or something far worse.

We give thanks each day that our daughter has no major medical problems, and we know how much more difficult our lives could be if we had those sorts of issues to contend with on top of everything else. Thinking this way can sometimes put things in perspective and help you to appreciate what you have.

CELEBRATING PROGRESS, NOT PERFECTION
Don't overlook even the smallest victories

A critical strategy, which may seem very difficult at times, is to stop comparing our children to other typically developing kids, and instead to look at their progress as individuals. Michey and I learned this very important concept some time ago from Dan Sullivan through The Strategic Coach Program; it has proven invaluable in helping us not only to cope but to have a much more positive attitude.

Every parent has hopes and dreams that their lives will unfold in certain ways. For us parents of children with special needs, it is easy to look at other kids and families and think of how life could have been, and to lament how far behind and different our children seem in comparison.

While we may never overcome all the feelings of loss, jealousy or inequality, we can make choices about how we deal with our situations to gain a more positive outlook and to help us to better appreciate what we have.

The reality of life is that every child is different, and typically developing children are no exception. Some kids naturally excel in certain areas, such as academics and sports, and other kids, no matter how hard they try, will never come close to matching the achievements of their exceptionally gifted peers. Middle-of-the-road children will always come up short if they are constantly compared to high achievers.

The same goes for our kids with special needs compared to other kids their age. We will never be able to appreciate the progress our children make if we keep comparing them to those with greater abilities. Our kids are individuals with unique qualities.

All progress, even the smallest steps, must be celebrated. Once we start looking at our children individually, and appreciate their personal milestones over time, we can enjoy and cherish their accomplishments together with them.

To help you to record and celebrate your childrens' accomplishments each day, download Your Family Achievement Diary for free from Drive4Rebecca. org. Use this diary for all of your children and as time goes on, and you look back at everything, you will be astounded at all of their achievements.

SUMMARY

Take time for yourself and your significant other.

Make time for fun with friends and relatives, and ask for their help.

Don't forget that other people have issues, no matter how trivial they sound, because more than anyone we need our friends.

Celebrate your child's progress. Every achievement counts, no matter how small.

2
FINDING
BABYSITTERS

OVERVIEW

You can't do it all yourself and you need a break.

If money is an issue, ask friends and relatives to get involved or pursue other free options.

How to find the best possible help to make sure your child is safe.

SCREENING AND HIRING THE BEST BABYSITTERS
You need to find the best possible help

Finding people to help you with your children is a very sensitive issue, especially if like our daughter Rebecca, your child does not communicate and cannot tell you if someone is not taking care of them properly or, worse, if someone is hurting them. It all comes down to trust, and trusting your own instincts. It also helps to thoroughly check references because you can find out a lot of information about people if you ask the right questions and if you are open about your situation.

Some individualized education programs include after-school tutoring, and there are state-sponsored respite programs and private foundations that can help pay for aides. If you are lucky enough to have family nearby you can also ask your relatives to help, or you can seek help from friends. You may also be able to work out something with other families who have children with special needs by taking turns having them watch your children and you watching theirs either overnight or for the weekend.

We found one of our first babysitters through an ad in the newspaper, and she worked with our daughter on and off for many years. Subsequently, several of her friends babysat many times. More recently we found that the reliability of having live-in help was a big improvement over dealing with the shifting schedules of college kids and constantly having to find new people (and it has been really nice to have help first thing in the morning).

We have developed a system that has worked very well when we have been looking for new babysitters. The first thing to do is to figure out exactly what kind of help you need, and then write and place an advertisement in local newspapers (see Appendix for our ad). You may also want to send requests to local college job placement offices, and to teaching departments and colleges that have occupational, speech and physical therapy programs. For live-in help, some people we know have had a lot of success with au pair agencies, and others have had mixed results. One family went through three individuals and significant damage to one of their cars (the au pair ran into a retaining wall while backing out of the driveway) before finding the right person. We were lucky to have friends from Utah who helped us find someone from their hometown and then guided us on how to advertise and hire recent high school graduates and college students. While we have had our fair share of interesting babysitter situations, so far we have had two live-in babysitters that have been terrific.

Rather than using your home phone number, try to set up a voice mailbox on another line or use voice mail on a cell phone, and record a message to help weed out poor candidates. That way you do not have to be bothered at home, especially because you never know who will call, and you can prescreen from the messages, deleting those that do not sound good or that do not answer the question posed on your voice mail recording. (See Appendix for our voice mail message asking candidates to describe why they feel they are the best person for the job.) I once read in a sales magazine about a similar method being used to prescreen potential salespeople. You would be surprised by some of the responses we have received. Some omitted important information like a telephone number, a few spent a lot of time mentioning God, and others simply did not answer the question at all. We feel that things are difficult enough already for Rebecca. We do not want to even consider anyone who does not listen, does not communicate well, or cannot follow the very simple instructions that we leave on our recording. (Alternatively, email is also a good way to start, and you can ask for a resume and references.)

Once you hear voice mail messages that sound promising, call those individuals and ask a number of questions over the telephone (see Appendix for telephone interview questions), tell them about your child and the job, and if they seem to be a good match, ask for three or more references. When checking references, we try to find out as much as possible about the candidate, sometimes asking the same questions in different ways.

Recently we have had good luck with a web site called Nannies4Hire.com. You post a detailed job description and receive email from applicants who are interested in the position. Most candidates provide photographs, height, weight and detailed information about their experience. You can often determine a lot about their level of education and mastery of the English language from the way they write about themselves. Weight is important to us because we want someone who can be physical and keep up with Rebecca — running alongside her when she is on her bike, for example. It is also essential that the person can communicate clearly; we need to hire someone who will understand what Rebecca needs and how to help her most effectively and keep her safe.

CHECK REFERENCES, THOROUGHLY
Many people lie

You should ask for as many references as you can get until you feel comfortable. We consider references from friends or family members to be questionable and not very reliable. Ask references how they know the babysitter (is it a relative, a friend of the family, etc.), and ask if there was anything, even a small thing, that they did not like or that bothered them about the babysitter. (See Appendix for reference questions.) Mention that you have a child with special needs and how important it is to find someone you can trust (which is particularly important if your child, like Rebecca, does not communicate).

We have found that some references do not want to give out too much information, or are not very enthusiastic about the candidate, especially references from non- babysitting jobs such as restaurants or retail stores. When checking this sort of reference, one question that can be very revealing is, "Would you feel comfortable having this person watch your kids, or your nephews or nieces?" That sometimes elicits a simple yes or no answer, or a moment of thoughtful silence, and that is often all you need to hear.

Sometimes we have gotten startling information from references. Once, after we had spoken to a woman on the phone, asking a number of questions and explaining how important it was for us to have someone we can trust, she called back to tell us that the babysitter had hit her child "across the face" and that that was why the babysitter was not working for her anymore. The grandmother of another potential babysitter seemed surprised by our questions and said, "She wants to babysit? I have ten other grandchildren that could babysit, but I don't know about her." Another person, when asked about a babysitter, replied, "She never worked for me and I'm not going lie for her anymore." While there truly are some gems in this world, some people sound too good to be true and those individuals who have something to hide are often the ones that make up the most intricate stories.

Once we are satisfied with the references, and if the candidate sounds terrific, we schedule a time to meet, or set up a videoconference if the person is out of state (very easy with computers these days, using Skype or iChat or even a local Apple store), and we essentially ask many of the same questions again to reconfirm the answers (see Appendix for interview questions). You will sometimes find that the new answers do not match the original ones. If the candidate does not have a good explanation, that is usually a clear signal to keep the interview brief and tell the person that you will be in touch if you are interested. If we are meeting in person, we also observe how the babysitter interacts with Rebecca and whether or not she seems to feel comfortable with her.

Finally, when you find someone who seems great, and if they are local, invite them to spend some time with your family, as a paid trial for training and as a way to assess how well it goes with your kids. We have been very fortunate in that many babysitters have stayed on with us for quite some time and have become like big sisters to Rebecca.

ASK RELATIVES AND FRIENDS
Don't be afraid to request babysitting help

Don't be shy – ask people to help out with babysitting. If you have relatives in the area, they should be the first people you ask because they are familiar with your child. If not, ask your close friends. Our twin nieces took a local babysitting course when they were fifteen that included first aid training. As a result they gained more confidence which made it easier for them to take care of Rebecca. You may also be able to find other families who have a child with special needs and work out an arrangement to take turns babysitting every so often so you can all have a break.

COMMUNITY SERVICE HELP
Free help from terrific kids

We found out that many high schools require or encourage community service, and in some cases it is an option for students to earn school credits in lieu of attending classes.

We called some local high schools and spoke to the staff members in charge of coordinating community service. We explained that we could use volunteers in a variety of situations, including as helping hands around the house after school, during Girl Scout meetings, and on weekends for family outings. We wrote a letter that was circulated in the schools (see Appendix for sample letter), and a number of students responded that they were interested in working with Rebecca.

Each of these student volunteers spent time in our home learning how to work with Rebecca, following our lead and receiving guidance from therapists and babysitters. A number of these terrific kids have assisted Rebecca when we have spent time together as a family, in extracurricular activities, and in school-year vacation programs at our local community center. Two of the students became paid babysitters over the summer and continued to help during the school year after they had completed their community service obligations. There is a constant supply of these wonderful kids, and those that are interested in community service can be a great help in many situations.

SUMMARY

Everyone needs a break.

Make sure you have the best person to watch your child.

Can't afford babysitting? Friends and family members can help and you can seek out resources in the community.

3
IN THE COMMUNITY

OVERVIEW

How to include your child in everything you do, including recreational activities and trips to places like Disneyland.

Some things are harder to do than others, but there are many ways around the obstacles.

Including your child in mainstream activities can take time, lots of planning, finding the right people who want to help, and sometimes going up against the status quo, but it's worth it.

SPENDING TIME IN PUBLIC PLACES
It is worth the hard work

One of the greatest challenges for many families is taking their children to public places. It often takes a lot of time and practice for children with special needs to get acclimated to new places and situations. Unfortunately, some children and families never get a chance to succeed because after one exasperating experience they never again venture out in public together. You take your child somewhere and he or she makes a big fuss. Everyone stares, you feel embarrassment or shame, and your heart starts pounding. Some people make nasty or insensitive comments and make you feel really bad about your heroic attempt at normalcy. So you refrain from trying again. It can divide families because one parent stays home while the other takes the rest of the kids to public places. But try not to let that rough first outing hold you and you child back. Give it some time.

For me, it is more of an annoyance, rather than an embarrassment, when Rebecca is crying or being difficult in public. I sometimes feel really badly for her. She has no other way of communicating and must be really frustrated sometimes when her dad is dragging her all over the place. She may have a headache, she may be hungry, or she simply may not be in the mood for whatever it is we are doing, but she has no way of telling me except by crying or trying to get out of the situation.

ASKING FOR HELP
People will help

It has always been relatively easy for me to take Rebecca places because I am not very concerned with what other people think about her behavior. I'm too busy focusing on keeping her safe, calm and happy. In fact, when people stare I sometimes just give a really big wave and a loud, friendly "hello," and that usually is the end of it.

One time I was with Rebecca in a very casual self-service seafood restaurant in City Island, New York. It was a juggling act just getting all the food and drinks and Rebecca situated in a booth. Just when it looked like things were going really well, I dropped her straw on the ground. She was not very good at drinking out of a cup at the time, but I couldn't leave her in the booth while I got a new straw because she might get up and walk away. And if I got up and took her with me, she might think it was time to leave and then it would be difficult to get her to sit quietly again to eat. I noticed a little boy staring at Rebecca, so I enlisted his help. I asked him if he could grab a straw for us. He was off and running, and came back in a few seconds, and all was well. (In general, I have found that kids are much more helpful and understanding than adults are.)

iPOD AND iPHONE ENTERTAINMENT
Technology to the rescue

Buying a video iPod was one of the best investments we ever made. Years ago I had a video camcorder, and a friend with a video duplicating company transferred Rebecca's favorite videos onto camcorder tapes. I bought a tiny Sony television that I could connect to the camcorder, but I had my hands full just trying to play a video.

We bought a portable DVD player when prices came down and that was a big improvement, but it was still a hassle. We always had to carry a selection of DVDs, and often had to swap them to find one that Rebecca wanted to watch at that moment. Some disks invariably got damaged. Eventually the DVD player dropped and broke, but we did get a few good years out of it.

When the video iPod came out I knew I had found the perfect solution, and it has proven to be invaluable in so many situations. We have used it in restaurants, in doctors' waiting rooms, in airports, and on airplanes. Essentially, it has been indispensable practically anywhere we have needed to keep Rebecca entertained.

We have even been able to let Rebecca watch videos discreetly, without sound, at bar and bat mitzvahs while she sits with us for extended periods of time.

And now that I own an iPhone, I have all of Rebecca's videos in my pocket at all times, as well as all of her favorite songs. As they say in the Visa commercials, "priceless."

DADS IN THE LADIES ROOM
Avoiding gross men's rooms

If you are a dad and are fortunate to have a daughter, you gain the privilege of being able to take your little girl to single-person ladies rooms.

I can assure you from a great deal of personal experience that women's bathrooms are far cleaner than men's bathrooms, so take advantage of this little perk. Sometimes when emerging from the bathroom I have been greeted by women with puzzled looks on their faces. When I point to my little lady they quickly realize what's going on, and I have never had a problem.

FIND SPECIAL-NEEDS-FRIENDLY PEOPLE AND PLACES
There are so many welcoming people out there

Several years ago Rebecca would frequently wake up at or before 6am, and when

I tried to get her back to sleep she would cry or make a lot of noise. To keep the peace and avoid waking up the rest of the family, the only choice I had was to leave the house with her and go somewhere. We took walks or went places that were open early, like a local diner or Starbucks.

One morning Tommy Sherwood, the manager at the Starbucks, came up to me when I was reading books to Rebecca. He said he had seen us on many early mornings and wanted to learn how he and his associates could be more helpful to people with special needs. He took the time to ask a lot of questions, especially because he was starting a family. That Starbucks location became one of my favorite destinations with Rebecca, since I knew that the staff would be welcoming, friendly and helpful.

Tommy and I became friends, and he helped with many fund-raising events. One day he called and was very excited to share some news. He had hired Chris, a young adult with autism and he said he never would have hired Chris if he hadn't gotten to know Rebecca. He later told me that Chris ended up being one of his best employees because of his great memory, his attention to detail, and his great sense of humor.

PRACTICE MAKES PERFECT
Try, try again

We have learned that, with practice, Rebecca can handle practically any situation, and that is the case with many children. It takes time, a lot of patience on our part, and the help of kind people in the community. Look for loud restaurants where your noise won't be very noticeable, or become a regular at places where you know the staff is friendly. Introduce yourself to the owner or manager and explain your situation. You will be pleasantly surprised that, more often than not, people are sympathetic, warm and welcoming, and they truly want to help.

In many circumstances we have rehearsed over and over with Rebecca to help her become as comfortable as possible before an important event. For example, for her cousins' bar and bat mitzvahs and for her own, we went to temple once or twice a week, either during a service or when the chapel was empty, to help familiarize her with the room. We brought along her books, snacks and video iPod. In all three instances, when it came time for the actual event she did great. We also try to arrive early for special events so that if Rebecca is a little cranky at first it does not disturb everyone or draw a lot of attention. She generally settles down after a few minutes, and on many occasions has been able to sit quietly for several hours at a time. There are times that Rebecca is unhappy despite our best efforts. For the most part however, with the right kind of preparation, things seem to work out very well.

We once discussed our situation with the manager of a local movie theater, and he let us take Rebecca to early shows that were not crowded. He agreed that if she wasn't able to last very long he would give us our money back, and said that we could return and keep practicing until she was successful.

Our friends Faye and Glen spent a lot of time getting their son Max, who has autism, to feel comfortable spending time in a local restaurant. Eventually they became friendly with the manager, Bobbie, who was always nice to Rebecca whenever we stopped by. Bobbie, who had no children of his own, was so taken with Max that he volunteered to provide after-school vocational training to Max at his restaurant.

There are countless restaurants and other business establishments out there. Call ahead to request any special accommodations that might make things easier for you. Rebecca is better in booths and by windows and we sometimes call when we are on the way to a restaurant to see if those tables are available. If you are going to choose where to spend your hard-earned money, make sure that it is appreciated and that you are treated kindly, because you deserve it more than anyone.

RECREATIONAL ACTIVITIES
There are many programs available for your child

When we were originally told that Rebecca might not walk until age three or four, we never imagined that with some assistance she would one day be able to ride horses, roller-blade, bike ride, ice-skate, swim, and even ski. Never say never. We can strive for our kids to do everything that other kids can do — things that the other kids and their parents usually take for granted.

We have learned that there are many terrific special programs in almost every activity you can imagine. We found a therapeutic horseback-riding program in our area where Rebecca gained the confidence to ride, improved her balance, and really enjoyed herself. She also enjoys an occasional pony ride which is usually much less expensive than therapeutic riding.

A few years ago, another couple reported in an online discussion group that their son, who has the same disorder as Rebecca has, had gone skiing a few times and was starting to turn the skis on his own. As an avid skier myself, I was intrigued. I had never even considered the idea that Rebecca would be able to ski.

I did some research and found out about a well-established adaptive skiing program within two hours of our home called The Adaptive Sports Foundation at Windham Mountain, in Windham, New York. It is called adaptive skiing because the program adapts the skiing experience to the abilities of the individual. (There are similar programs around the country, and we have also had great experiences at the National Ability Center in Park City, Utah.) There are skiers with a variety of special needs, including some without legs and — one of the most amazing things I have ever seen — skiers who are blind, who descend a slope surrounded by volunteers in bright orange vests. You know a blind skier is coming when you hear one of the volunteers shouting "Left! Right!" It is a remarkable program, and the volunteers are some of the nicest people you will ever meet.

At Windham, more than 100 professionally trained volunteers assist skiers, and the program is subsidized by a foundation to keep the cost relatively low for participants. (It costs $60 for two hours in the morning and two hours in the afternoon, including lift ticket, skis, boots, poles, and any adaptive equipment.) Rebecca enjoys skiing, and I am confident that in time she will be able to ski on her own. And because of the program, we are able to ski together as a family. Some of the skiers in the program are really fast and you should hear them cheer as they cross the finish line during the race at the end of the season.

There are also ice hockey leagues for kids with special needs, and our town has a wonderful Challenger Sports league with soccer and baseball. It is a terrific inclusion program where typically developing kids volunteer to play with the children with special needs. We started taking Rebecca roller-skating when she was very young because the local rink allowed adults without skates to help their children. That made it much easier for her learn how to skate, and as a result of seeing how much she enjoyed it her school decided to teach all of the kids. Many of them are incredible skaters. The rink where she skated had a volunteer who coached kids for a Special Olympics skating competition. Go to Special-Olympics.org to learn more about all of their wonderful programs.

GETTING TO THE FRONT OF THE LINE
If you can't wait, you may not have to

When we visit friends and relatives in California, Disneyland is one of our all-time favorite places to go with Rebecca. Disneyland offers a pass for people with special needs that enables us to go right to the front of the line on most rides and attractions (usually by entering through the exit). Since Rebecca does not have a lot of patience, our experience at Disney was great. We avoided really long lines that would have been very difficult for Rebecca and for us, and we were able to go on many more rides than we could have without the pass. We joke with friends and family that Rebecca is available to join them when they take a trip to the Magic Kingdom.

In general, if your child has difficulty waiting, when you find a very long line you should find the person who is in charge and, accompanied by your child, explain your situation and politely ask if there is any way to avoid waiting. Most people will be very accommodating once they understand your situation. When we encountered a one-hour wait to go to the top of the Empire State Building, the security workers were very nice and let us go to the front of the line.

MAKING DOCTOR VISITS A LITTLE EASIER
Plan ahead and call on your way

A strategy to avoid unnecessary waiting at doctors' offices is to call in advance and ask them to fax or email any forms. That way you can fill out everything before you arrive and you won't have to juggle completing the paperwork with taking care of your child and keeping him or her entertained. It will make it much easier for you to focus on your child without extra stress, in a situation that is already potentially stressful.

In addition, if your child has a difficult time waiting at the doctor's office, call before you arrive to see if they are running on time. Explain your situation so they understand why you need to know. If they are behind schedule, you can take a walk or relax for a while in the car, and then call again for an update. Trying to get the doctor's first appointment of the day can also help you avoid long waits. Ask them to call in any prescriptions to your pharmacy to avoid even more waiting.

While Rebecca is able to wait in many situations — and it can be a good learning experience — there are times when we find it especially important to avoid waiting, if possible. For example, when we take a vacation as a family, having to wait in long lines at the airport with a cranky Rebecca is not the best way to start our trip. We usually pay a little extra to check in our bags at curbside because it makes things so much easier. And we have been allowed to go through special lines to avoid long waits for security screenings, which really makes a difference.

INCLUSION OPPORTUNITIES
Good for all children

Inclusion means including children with special needs in situations together with typically developing kids. It is especially important because there are not always many options for inclusion and there are so many benefits for children with special needs and their families, and for typically developing children as well. Inclusive situations allow for great learning experiences, as children with special needs gain exposure to the age-appropriate behaviors of typically developing peers rather than being limited to interactions with similarly affected children. And mainstream children can learn important lessons about differences between people, tolerance, and acceptance of others.

We have found that the more people that get to know Rebecca in our community, the greater the likelihood that those we encounter will be nice to her rather than being scared or unsure of how to react when they see her waving her arms around or making funny sounds.

We have had success with inclusion in Girl Scouts, in local community center programs, and in summer camp. Rebecca has attended Girl Scouts for years, with the help of an aide, a community service volunteer, or a babysitter. The other girls in the troop have gained an understanding of Rebecca and are nice to her, and she has generally enjoyed herself whether or not she is able to participate in all of the activities.

While having troop leaders with exceptionally good attitudes was pivotal in making Girl Scouts a success for Rebecca, we also owe a great deal of debt to the special needs director at the JCC of Greater Washington at the time Rebecca was starting out. She gave us great advice on how to bring Rebecca into the Girl Scouts and taught us terrific sensitivity exercises (see Appendix) that we used in an introductory session with the troop, without Rebecca present. That meeting helped provide the girls with a greater understanding of why Rebecca is the way she is, how Rebecca is different from them (non-verbal), and the many ways that she is the same (likes peanut butter and jelly, swimming, videos, laughing, etc.). We used the same exercises with great success in many recreational programs at our local community center.

INCLUSION AT ITS BEST
Kids can be so kind

As a result of Rebecca's involvement with Girl Scouts, we had a really special experience when she was very young that I will never forget. While we were having dessert at a local bakery, her fellow Girl Scout Ella walked in with her dad, saw Rebecca, and wanted to sit next to her, but there was only one seat available. When her father said they needed to go to the back of the bakery because there wasn't enough room, Ella told her dad to go without her because she wanted to sit with her friend. It was heartwarming that another child had learned to be kind to Rebecca rather than being scared of her or even making fun of her. For children with special needs it can only be good to have more people in the community understand them and treat them with kindness, and for the other kids who get to know them it is a terrific learning experience (it can also help their parents to be more sensitive and understanding).

Another time that we experienced the benefits of inclusion was when my brother and sister-in-law brought Rebecca to watch her cousin's soccer game. A little girl named Charlotte came up to her and said hello. When my brother asked how they knew each other, Charlotte said, "Rebecca is my friend from camp." Because Charlotte and Rebecca changed in the locker room for swimming at the same time each day, Charlotte got to know her and felt she was a friend. Since Charlotte knew what to expect when she saw Rebecca, instead of asking her parents why Rebecca made "funny noises" she just came right up to Rebecca to say hello. That is what inclusion is all about.

The time Rebecca has spent on a regular basis with typically developing children, with all of the related commotion and noise, has helped her deal more successfully with similar social situations like birthday parties, restaurant outings, and holiday dinners.

While there are many opportunities for inclusion, you sometimes have to work really hard to create new ones and to get others to buy in. Some people are initially resistant, but they often come around when they see the benefits both for your child and for the rest of the children. My wife and I fought for Rebecca to be included in summer camp after the camp told us "she doesn't belong here." After a great deal of time and effort on our part, and with the help of some caring people in the community, Rebecca's camp has made good progress with inclusion. They planned more activities — such as swimming, lunch, and special events — in ways that allowed campers with special needs to be included with mainstream kids. With new staff and new attitudes, they have come a long way.

FROM INCLUSIONFORALL.ORG
Supporting summer camp inclusion
The following information is from InclusionForAll.org, a web site I created after our fight to get Rebecca included in camp. Use this information to help guide you if you are having trouble getting your child included in any situation.

Many People Want to Help
There are many people who want to help make sure that your child has a fun and fulfilling summer, and will do whatever it takes to make it happen.

Some People Will Stand in Your Way
At the same time, you may encounter some people who, for whatever reason — fear of the unknown, fear of change, or simply ignorance — do not want to include your child or other children with special needs in their regular programs.

The ADA Protects People With Disabilities
While the best first road to take is to find people in the community who can help you, in many situations you also have the law on your side — The Americans with Disabilities Act (ADA), enforced by the U.S. Department of Justice, offers protections for people with disabilities.

Be Persistent — Don't Give Up!
Nothing is more important than your persistence. Everyone is busy, and everyone has different priorities. Your persistence will help make your child a higher priority. If you feel you personally do not have the strength to do it, find a friend or family member to help you.

Use All Available Resources

Your school, and local community service organizations like The Arc, may be able to provide you and your camp with guidance, training and professional support on inclusion. Teachers, behaviorists and other professionals may be available to provide on-site assistance.

Contact Board Members, Trustees and Founders

Board members and trustees can help you if you encounter difficulties in getting your child included in a program. They are the most important donors who have the most influence. Do not be shy about calling them. You can get their names, and possibly their telephone numbers, from staff members or from an annual report. Or look for names on large commemorative plaques. When I called one older board member and she heard about the obstacles we had faced in getting Rebecca included in camp, she actually started crying and said "your little girl will be included in camp" and our problems were quickly solved.

Gain Strength From Challenges and Seek Help From Others

While no one will be a stronger advocate than you, if you ask around and seek out the right people, you will find that there are many caring individuals who want to help you and your child. Do not give up. Try to gain strength from the challenges you face. Your child deserves it.

SUMMARY

You can take your child with you wherever you and your family go.

People want to help and will do so if you ask.

Practice, practice more, and keep on practicing.

Be confident and assertive in making sure your child can participate with your family and in your community.

4
YOUR HEALTH

OVERVIEW

You must take care of yourself.

Don't put off taking care of your mental and physical health.

It is essential to be as healthy and strong as possible — in mind, body and spirit — for you and your family to survive and thrive.

WHAT DOESN'T KILL YOU MAKES YOU STRONGER
This doesn't necessarily apply to our lives

When you are taking care of individuals with special needs, sometimes you feel beaten down and just run out of steam. This life can beat you down, and it can destroy your marriage and your relationships, if you are not careful and don't take care of yourself. The good news is there are things we can do to survive and even thrive in spite of all of the challenges and hardships we face each day.

It is vital — I repeat, VITAL — that you take care of yourself and make sure you are in the best possible health physically, emotionally, psychologically and spiritually.

To make it through each day, you first need to determine how to take care of yourself. It is often hard to focus on yourself when you have to take care of someone with special needs (and maybe typically developing children as well) while dealing with all of the day-to-day responsibilities both inside and outside your home. But you must.

GETTING SOME HELPFUL ADVICE
Find a "relationship coach"

Michey and I have gone to what I call a "relationship coach" (a therapist) several times over the years when we have run into rough spots during particularly stressful times or when we are just not being very kind to each other. We have addressed all sorts of issues, and while the advice we have received has often been very simple and maybe should have been obvious, it has nonetheless been a big help.

While counseling can be expensive, it can be a critically important survival strategy when things get really tough. Many insurance policies have coverage for counseling, and many large companies and community nonprofit organizations have free or low-cost programs that provide short-term counseling and referral services.

If money is an issue, you can seek advice from your clergy person (we have spoken to our rabbi) or try to find a sympathetic close friend or family member who you feel will not be judgmental or take sides. If you have a dog, you can try another option (no, I don't mean talking to your dog but if you find that helps why not). When we lived in New York City and would go to the dog run, for some reason people who were almost complete strangers seemed to feel comfortable talking about nearly anything. Maybe the dogs somehow relaxed people and removed some of their inhibitions. I told all sorts of things to people whom I hardly knew, and it was amazing what some people told me. It was very strange now that I look back at it, but it certainly did no harm and may have helped in some way, even by just allowing me to get things off my chest.

Just talking through some of the very difficult issues in life, especially with someone who is looking in from the outside, can often make you feel better, and the other person may be able to provide some ideas and solutions that would have never crossed your mind.

GETTING SOME SPIRITUALITY
Peace of mind is critical

When Rebecca was very young we started going to synagogue on a regular basis because we wanted her to become comfortable there and eventually to have some sort of bat mitzvah. We joined a particular congregation because they had been welcoming adults with special needs to their Saturday morning services for years and the Rabbi had a child with autism.

Rebecca became very comfortable and so did we, as we were welcomed into the temple community by a really nice group of people. Friday night services are a time to reflect on the week, to slow down, and to pray or just relax. Rebecca had a difficult time at first but eventually grew to really enjoy going to services. It was easy to be there, especially after a long week. The services were casual and only forty-five minutes long, which was perfect for us.

GETTING OFF YOUR LAZY BUTT
Just get a little exercise

OK, so maybe it's not laziness. You are truly wiped out and don't have one ounce of energy left. You need that pint of Ben & Jerry's to make you feel better after getting yelled at by your spouse while one child was having a tantrum and your other child was misbehaving. Basically everything that can possibly go wrong has gone wrong.

You also may feel that you don't have the time to exercise between taking care of your kids, going to work, and attending to never-ending household chores and other commitments. Not to mention that your strength is sapped by the occasional emergency visits to doctors and hospitals, running to school to pick up your kids when they think something is wrong, or when something is really wrong, and being woken up frequently during the night. I know all about these things from personal experience, but I have made exercise one of my top priorities.

No matter how busy you are, how stressful life feels at the moment, and how impossible it seems to fit it in, if you don't figure out how to get some exercise you will only make your situation more difficult as time goes by. In the words of a wise older gentleman whom I used to see all the time riding his bicycle when we lived in New York City, "you have to make the time to take the time." It really doesn't matter what you do; what is important is that you do some type of exercise to increase your heart rate and strength and that you make it part of your routine.

I have made a concerted effort to combine exercise and spending time with Rebecca for example, by taking long walks together, running with her in her Baby Jogger or now in her larger Independence Push Chair, or pulling her behind my bicycle in a bike trailer. All of these activities help me stay physically active while I'm enjoying quality time with my daughter.

And because I have gotten into the habit of exercising nearly every day, at 45 years old I am probably in the best shape of my life, despite the fact that I love to eat (I could still benefit from losing some weight). I only started running a few years ago and now I run half marathons, swim a mile at a time, bike long distances, and just completed my first triathlon. Earlier in my life, the only time you might see me run was if someone was chasing me. I have also changed the way I eat, and Michey has helped in this area in a big way — she is a great cook and makes delicious and healthy meals, and the refrigerator is always stocked with fresh fruits and vegetables.

Staying in shape can work miracles for you psychologically and emotionally. And it will help your child, because you will be a better caregiver. If I don't stay in shape, Rebecca will become too much for me to handle. She reminds me of Steve Austin in The Six Million Dollar Man — she is getting bigger, faster and stronger — and I have to keep up. I have often read about how much of an impact stress can have on your life, and at times the stress levels in our lives are off the charts. I am certain that all of my exercise helps to counter the negative effects of stress in my life, and helps me get an escape and handle everything much better than if I didn't work out.

I do a lot of exercise — much more than almost anyone I know. Don't be intimidated and feel you need to do what I do. Just do something you enjoy a few days a week and gradually increase your level of activity. Anything is better than nothing.

EATING HEALTHIER
Healthy can taste good

Many years ago we heard someone speak about the evils of partially hydroge-nated oils. We figured that with all of Rebecca's problems we should probably try to eliminate them from her diet, and with Whole Foods Market nearby it was an easy thing to do. Although it was more expensive, we knew that we were eating healthier and that it would be good for our entire family.

Something else that was good for our health came about after a friend who is a cardiologist recommended that my wife and I take the Berkeley blood test, especially because she has a major cholesterol problem. The Berkeley blood test gives you much more comprehensive and useful information about cholesterol than typical blood tests do. The most helpful thing was that by taking the test we were entitled to meet with a nutritionist on a regular basis for free at Berkeley's local center (they have a few in North America — see 4myheart.com). What the nutritionist told me was not new: eat whole grains and lots of fruits and vegetables, and cut out as much white flour, pasta and rice as possible. What was new was that it finally got me to change the way I ate, and I lost more than ten pounds over several months. Maybe it was because we scheduled follow-up appointments, so I was accountable to someone.

I still have rice, white bread and pasta now and then, but less frequently. There is no way I will ever give up my triple chocolate Balthazar cookies, but I eat a lot fewer of those and much more of the better foods, which will help me keep off the excess weight and stay healthier.

YOU DON'T HAVE TO JOIN A GYM
Find something you like to do

With our crazy and hectic lives it is very difficult to find the time to exercise, but there are ways to do it, even together with your family. Taking family walks, going to nature centers, or even strolling through the mall early in the morning when the weather is bad are all good options. I discovered the mall-walking phenomenon several years ago when Rebecca was waking up every day at 6am and I needed to get her out of the house so she wouldn't wake up the rest of the family. I learned that many malls are open twenty-four hours a day and people meet there on a regular basis and walk together — especially older folks all decked out in their finest matching sweatsuits.

The time I have spent over the years with Rebecca just taking walks has been really special for me. It is something we can enjoy together anywhere we go, even before or after a doctor's appointment or in between errands. And since we live within walking distance of town and of a very nice park, we walk all the time.

Since Rebecca was a baby I have made time to get regular exercise either in a local gym at 5:30 in the morning or late at night after everyone is asleep. I used to take her for long rides in the bike trailer behind my bicycle until she got too big for it, but I will be getting a bigger one soon. Even now that Rebecca is fourteen years old and weighs over 70 pounds, I push her in the push chair while running up and down the hills in our neighborhood. I also have something called a trainer that attaches to the rear wheel of my bicycle and converts it into a stationary bike so I can exercise at home. There are so many ways to get exercise; you just need to find something that is right for you.

Dylan is a student in Rebecca's school who also has autism. His family figured out a really nice way to spend time together while getting exercise. When Dylan was very young he loved walking around his neighborhood. By the time he was three and a half years old, he had learned how to ride a bicycle with training wheels. The only problem was finding time to ride because he often had all-day therapy sessions starting at 8am. His parents decided to take him on 6:30am bike rides while they pushed his one-year-old brother in a jogging stroller. They were able to help Dylan build on his skills, spend quality time together as a family, and get exercise, all at the same time.

Michey has taken yoga classes for years for her own peace of mind, to get in better shape, and to enjoy the meditative aspects. To learn something new she enrolled in a yoga teacher training program at a local gym. After getting certified she started teaching yoga one day a week while continuing to take classes, and she got in great shape. If you haven't tried yoga and you're skeptical, it is not just sitting around and relaxing and saying "ohm." I have taken her 90-minute classes and they were some of the most challenging workouts I have ever had.

TAKE TIME FOR YOUR HEALTH
Or make time for illness

The bottom line is that we need to exercise and take care of our health if we want to be strong for, and enjoy time with, our kids with special needs and our typically developing children. Staying fit is important for anyone, but it is particularly vital for families with children with special needs, given all of the pressures we are constantly under and the strength we need to deal with all of the psychological and physical demands on our lives.

I once saw a sign in a doctors' office that really stuck with me: "Those who don't make time for health will have to make time for illness." While we can come up with all sorts of excuses why we are unable to exercise, such as lack of time, if you get really sick and are laid up in a hospital bed, all of a sudden you will have all the time in the world but won't be able to do much. Wouldn't it be better to spend that time now making yourself healthier and having fun with your friends and family, and then have more time down the road to do things you really enjoy? Think about it; you can make the choice. Put down that bag of chips, and get off your butt and exercise. When you are finished, sit down and relax, and reward yourself with a healthy snack (and some Ben & Jerry's).

SUMMARY

Your child is counting on you and you owe it to your-self and your family to be the best you can be. It is easy to declare defeat, allow your health to falter, and mourn your situation, but you can make a better choice and take care of yourself.

Do whatever you can, including seeking outside coun-seling, to maintain the most positive attitude.

Make the time to exercise and stay healthy and strong. You will need it to survive and thrive.

5
THE BEST DOCTORS

OVERVIEW

You need to find the best doctors for your child.

Don't compromise with a doctor who doesn't have a great attitude.

Finding kind, caring and compassionate doctors can take extra time and effort, but it is well worth it.

THE GOOD, THE BAD AND THE UGLY
They should be as ashamed of themselves

Many individuals with special needs have significant medical issues requiring frequent doctor visits, hospitalizations and major surgeries. Having dental work or orthodontia done can be quite stressful and might require sedation. For many families, paging doctors after hours, calling 911, and visits to emergency rooms are all-too-familiar activities. My family has had its fair share of all of the above, and in all likelihood we will continue to have these types of experiences with Rebecca for the rest of our lives.

These medical situations, with all of the associated emotions and anxieties, are stressful. What can make them either far easier or much more difficult to handle are the attitudes and bedside manners of doctors.

We have experienced the good, the bad and the ugly in the medical field, and have worked hard to avoid bad doctors at all costs. One of the first doctors we visited was a geneticist who was supposedly a top expert in her field. Based on her very limited knowledge of Rebecca's extremely rare disorder (there were only a handful of known cases at the time), she said without any emotion or empathy: "If you have any hopes of her having similar intelligence to either of you, it is doubtful, and she may never walk." Even if that were true, what an incredibly insensitive way to speak to parents. Fast forward to today, and Rebecca skates, skis and sometimes runs, and has learned many skills we never imagined possible.

Another winner of the most clueless doctor award was the geneticist who was never available to talk on the phone. He ended up leaving a message on our answering machine saying that on top of Rebecca's one-in-a-million genetic disorder, she had a second very rare condition that would cause her to have severe medical problems for the rest of her life. My wife was devastated. As it turned out, we found another geneticist who quickly realized that the first doctor read the wrong column on a report and that the second diagnosis was a mistake.

GET SECOND (OR THIRD) OPINIONS
Don't settle

You are in charge of the medical care for your child. You *must* demand explanations, seek out the best information, and have all of your questions answered so that you understand everything that is going on. If you have a friend or family member who is a doctor, particularly a specialist in the relevant area of medicine, reach out and ask for help. See if they know of the doctor you are using, if they can help you get a second opinion on a recommended course of action, or if they can guide you to another physician if you have any doubts about who you're working with. Even if your child is going to a pediatric urologist and you know an adult urologist, it is worth a call. It is helpful to get some additional guidance and reassuring to have an understanding and knowledgeable person as a sounding board.

Medical care is incredibly expensive, and it can be complicated and confusing. Often there are several treatment options to choose from, and sometimes surgeons recommend an operation just because surgery is their area of expertise.

When Rebecca was very young, two different doctors recommended major hip surgery because her feet turned in. The surgery would have been extremely difficult for our family for many reasons, but especially because it would have been nearly impossible to keep Rebecca off her feet during the long recovery. We have to give some credit to one of the surgeons, who suggested that it might help Rebecca if we got her on a bicycle and roller skates. A third doctor, who was by far the nicest and also had a great reputation, told us she didn't need the surgery at all. We avoided a very difficult experience that ended up being completely unnecessary in our case.

Physical therapy can be an alternative to knee surgery, and medications and dietary changes can be alternatives to gastrointestinal surgery. Don't just follow the recommendations of one doctor without considering other options, especially in complicated cases.

ONLY USE KIND, PATIENT AND CARING DOCTORS
You deserve kindness

Life with children with special needs can be an emotional rollercoaster ride, and insensitive doctors are an evil that can be avoided. And what a difference it makes when you have a kind, caring, patient and sensitive doctor. It took us some time to figure this out, but one of the most important lessons we learned from our experiences was that it is worth almost any effort to make sure you only have compassionate, considerate, competent and patient professionals working with you and your family. Our problems with unkind doctors came to an end when we began asking Rebecca's neurologist, Dr. Arnold Gold, founder of The Gold Foundation for Humanism in Medicine, to recommend every doctor we needed. Once you find compassionate doctors, always ask for their recommendations for other specialists.

We now look only for doctors with the best attitudes, which we consider just as important as having great reputations in their field.

SUMMARY

You have the right and the power to choose and to demand the best from medical professionals.

The best is measured by competence and compassion.

More than anyone, you deserve kindness from people who really care.

6
PLANNING FOR
THE FUTURE

OVERVIEW

Raising a child with special needs can be incredibly expensive and complex.

Many costs, such as childcare and certain medical expenses, are not covered by insurance, and you need to be prepared for the unexpected.

Financial planners and estate planning attorneys can provide guidance to help you secure your future and the future of your children.

LOOK INTO PUBLIC BENEFITS
Find out what is free

Check with your state division of disabilities and local advocacy organizations to determine if your child qualifies for any financial assistance, such as funds for respite, medical devices, home modifications, or other services. The Arc (www. thearc.org) has offices all around the country and can point you in the right direction to help get you started.

FINANCIAL PLANNING
Every little bit counts

While you may be living from paycheck to paycheck, it is important to figure out how to put aside money for the future and for unexpected expenses. Plan for the long term to the best of your abilities, even though some days it is hard to see past tomorrow.

Look for a financial planner, ideally one who works with families with children with special needs, to help you with your finances. If you have a friend or family member who is an accountant or financial planner, ask for their help.

A financial planner can help you figure out what your significant other and your children would need to cover living expenses if you were no longer around. Find out the cost of life insurance and buy term insurance as soon as possible because it is least expensive when you are young and healthy.

If your employer has a 401(k) plan, make sure you contribute something, especially if your company matches your contributions. That is free money that should not be passed up even if it seems like a small amount. It all adds up over time and everything helps.

HANDBOOK ABOUT YOUR CHILD
Keep everything in one place

When Rebecca was very young we were referred to a financial planner who specialized in helping families with children with special needs. He helped us figure out how to do some budgeting, save some money and recommended putting together a binder (see Appendix for a sample handbook) with everything there is to know about Rebecca. The binder includes medical history, allergies, medications, school information, therapies, doctors, IEP and all related correspondence and evaluations, emergency contact information, and her daily schedule, including after-school activities and directions.

The binder keeps all pertinent information about Rebecca in one place. It is a reference guide for anyone who watches the kids while we are away or who might need to care for them if something happened to either or both of us.

It is important to update the binder at least once a year. Keep it on your bookshelf or somewhere that is easily accessible and let other people know where it is in case of an emergency. If you have access to a scanner, scan the contents of the binder periodically and save it on your computer as a backup.

ESTATE PLANNING
Protect their future

Depending upon your financial situation, an estate planning attorney can help you with a will, with determining who will care for your children in accordance with your wishes, and with creating a special needs trust to help manage any funds available to your child with special needs. Until you meet with an attorney, go to Nolo.com and buy and download WillMaker to create a basic will. This will give you something to start with until you are able to meet with someone to get things done the right way. Two good sources for attorneys who specialize in estate planning issues are SpecialNeedsAnswers.com and Special-NeedsAlliance.org.

You and your significant other should spend some time thinking about who will care for your children when you are gone. You will need to speak with the people you would like to designate as guardians of your children and trustees to make sure you and they are comfortable with the idea of them serving in that capacity and to be certain they understand your wishes.

PLAN NOW TO AVOID PROBLEMS IN THE FUTURE
It gets more and more difficult as time goes on

While anything having to do with a child with special needs can be daunting, difficult and extremely costly, we have no choice but to deal with our situations in the best way we can.

If you ignore or put off looking closely at your finances and making appropriate plans for the future, your situation will become more and more difficult to manage over time. Take the time to do something now, even if it does not seem like an ideal moment, so you can get a head start and avoid or mitigate much bigger problems in the future.

SUMMARY

Do what you can even with limited resources to plan for the future.

Without planning, things will become much more difficult for you and your family as time goes by.

While it may seem like you are not doing much, it is better to do something than nothing so that you are moving in the right direction.

7

ADVOCATING
FOR YOUR CHILD

OVERVIEW

What to do when you have to fight the school district.

The good news is you don't have to do it alone and it doesn't have to cost a lot of money.

How to make sure your health insurance works for you and your family

The most important thing is to do everything you can to ensure the best possible future for your child.

IT ISN'T EASY
You don't have to do it alone

It's hard enough being a parent, let alone a caregiver of a child with special needs. After dealing with all of the challenges, sometimes there is little strength left to fight for what your child is entitled to receive in school.

Many people don't have the knowledge, strength or energy to be the most effective advocate for their child. And that's OK, because not everyone can do it. It is often exhausting just trying to make it through the day without a major crisis.

So what can an overwhelmed, sleep-deprived parent do? Don't worry and don't give up; there are people who can help and it doesn't have to cost you a fortune.

DO IT YOURSELF OR FIND SOMEONE TO HELP
Many people can help

Our children have rights, they are our responsibility, and they deserve the best possible intervention –At the very least, they deserve our best effort.

If you don't have the strength or ability to figure it all out for your child — and hardly anyone can figure out everything by themselves without guidance — find a friend or family member to help. Is someone in your family particularly good at getting things done, or good at research, or very persistent or outspoken? Ask that person to give you a hand. (Outspokenness may be especially useful if you are more on the quiet side.) If there is a lawyer in the family or you have a friend who is an attorney, pick up the phone and ask for their help. Many law firms require community service and they might be glad to do what they can for you.

SPEAK TO AN ATTORNEY OR A VOLUNTEER ADVOCATE
Find someone who is knowledgeable

If you can afford a consultation with an attorney who specializes in advocating on behalf of individuals with special needs, pay for a one-hour consultation to learn the rights of your child (go to COPAA.org to find someone in your area). Otherwise, seek out a volunteer advocate in your community. You may be able to find such a person through a local social service agency or an organization such as The Arc.

We have generally had very good experiences and a friendly relationship with the Department of Special Services in our town. Early on someone advised us to speak with an attorney to better understand the law and to find out the best way to approach our school district when working on developing Rebecca's educational program. Our children are entitled to the most "appropriate" education and while that can be ambiguous and lead to disagreements it is important to know what services to request for your child and how to go about doing it. We never told our district that we had hired an attorney. Perhaps they figured it out because of the way we approached them and because we understood what to ask for and how to ask for it on behalf of Rebecca. We brought a tape recorder to some of our early meetings and said that a friend had suggested it so that we wouldn't have to take extensive notes and we could be more attentive. Actually we brought the tape recorder on the recommendation of the attorney. It put the school district officials on notice that we had a record of our conversations and gave us greater comfort that they would do the right thing for our family.

The lawyer proved invaluable over time and we never paid another fee for our periodic telephone consultations. She answered questions about various issues that came up and gave us great advice on the proper language to use with the school district when asking for specific services, and on how the law protected Rebecca. I am not sure if she was just being nice or if attorneys will do that because most of their income is derived from lawsuits. But you may find that you can get some free telephone advice from a lawyer once you have established a relationship, and if you end up having to go to court that person will be there and will be familiar with your situation.

JUST DIAGNOSED? RESEARCH LOCAL SCHOOL OPTIONS
Take the time to look around

It is all very confusing to try to figure out what to do educationally, especially in the beginning when your child is first diagnosed, when you are filled with emotions about your situation and may not know which way is up. The regulations governing special education have been written by bureaucrats and it takes a certain level of understanding to figure out all of the law's complexities.

One thing you can do when your child is first diagnosed is to look for a town that is special-education-friendly. We found that New Jersey towns all handle special education differently. We looked around and identified a town that had a reputation for being more cooperative with parents than others, and our experience over the years has confirmed that fact.

When we were unable to find an appropriate program for Rebecca that could accommodate her, we were very fortunate to have been able to join together with a number of other families in our area to help establish a school for children affected by autism called REED Academy. There were very few options available to us at the time and the only programs that looked like a good match were very small and had waiting lists in the hundreds. When we approached the directors of those schools and asked what it would take to start a new program, they were happy to put us in touch with other families in a similar situation and were glad to help us create a new program that would take some of the pressure off of their schools.

We know many families who have had to sue their school districts, including some of the families with whom we worked to establish Rebecca's school. Take the time to do some research and find out whatever you can about educational policies and procedures in your community or a community that you are exploring. Many towns have parent groups that meet about special education issues. Speak to parents with older children and find out what their experiences have been. If there are private special education school programs in your area, ask the program's directors for their opinions on which towns are easier to work with.

To avoid an expensive lawsuit, some people faced with a difficult school district may need to consider moving somewhere that is more special-education-friendly, more cooperative, and less combative.

DON'T BE LULLED INTO COMPLACENCY
School officials represent the town, not your child

Even though school officials may sincerely seem to care about your child, they have a built-in conflict of interest. While they are supposed to do what is most "appropriate" for each child, "appropriate" can be interpreted in many different ways. These officials may be nice people and have the best intentions, but the reality is that they are probably overworked and underpaid, and they ultimately are supposed to minimize costs for the school district. While appropriate can mean placement for a child in either a public or private program that is paid for with public funds, school districts will often lean towards doing whatever they can to save money.

Do not rely solely on what school officials recommend, and always seek out independent expert advice from therapists, developmental pediatricians, behavioral psychologists, and other professionals. Sometimes you need to go with your gut if something doesn't feel right — and don't delay seeking an independent evaluation if you are uncomfortable with a school district assessment or decision. If you sense something is wrong when your child is very young, there is nothing to be gained by waiting. The sooner you figure out what is needed, the sooner your child will get the right kind of help.

We learned the hard way about listening to the advice of our school district.

When our daughter was four, a behavioral psychologist gave her a diagnosis of having autistic tendencies. He recommended that she receive an educational program using a method called Applied Behavioral Analysis (ABA) and suggested a few private, not-for-profit programs in our area. After we shared this information with our educational team, they told us that the programs using ABA could not meet her needs, and instead suggested a public county school for children with autism. Since we didn't know any better, we just followed their recommendations and trusted them to do the right thing. Maybe they didn't know either.

We soon realized that the public school had very limited resources, and the staff was inadequately trained and had little, if any, access to leading edge curricula. The expensive consultant who was hired by the school district at our request was unable to make a difference because Rebecca's aide did not follow his recommendations (she was a union employee and must have had a high degree of job security). We eventually took it upon ourselves to visit the local private school programs and it was like night and day compared with Rebecca's school. We also discovered that the private schools were very small and had long waiting lists. We became painfully aware that we lost crucial time for early learning, and Rebecca was languishing and possibly regressing due to the substandard and inappropriate intervention she was receiving. We didn't know if the district made the recommendation to save money or if they just gave the wrong advice because of Rebecca's very unique disorder, but either way we knew we had to find something better.

Ultimately, together with a few other families and with the help of one of the local private schools we had visited, REED Academy opened. The school was identical to the programs our town originally deemed inappropriate and the results Rebecca achieved were stunning. In the first three months at REED Academy she learned far more than she had in the preceding three years. To their credit, our school district has been very supportive of REED Academy from day one and another child from town is enrolled in the school. Ironically, due to the inefficiency of the county program, Rebecca's total educational costs were significantly lower at REED Academy.

YOU ARE THE MOST PASSIONATE VOICE FOR YOUR CHILD
Speak up for your child

While it is not easy to start a new program and not everyone can do it, it is important to fight for the best educational options for your child. Even if you do get someone to help you advocate for your child, you ultimately will need to step up to the plate as the voice of your child. You should have someone strong by your side to help you, but no one will be more passionate than you.

Do not be bullied and don't let people push you around. Do not feel bad about stating your case strongly and being proactive on behalf of your child. The system is stacked against us because school districts know the law and have specialized attorneys on retainer. In order to keep expenses down, they may not go out of their way to provide anything more than the minimum level of services that could be interpreted by a court as "appropriate."

School districts have the upper hand. They have great resources available to them and the advantage of not having any emotional considerations affecting their decision-making process. They know the law, they have expensive lawyers at their disposal, and whatever the outcome, it ultimately comes down to dollars and cents to them. We parents, on the other hand, have huge emotional investments that can make it more difficult when advocating for our children whose lives are literally at stake based upon our actions and our ability to advocate successfully on their behalf. While life can be tough at times and incredibly tiring, find the strength to keep fighting for your child to get every possible service he or she is entitled to and deserves, even if it means ruffling some feathers.

If you are unable to reach a resolution with school officials that you and your advisors feel is right for your child, you may have to consider a lawsuit. This can be extremely costly, both financially and emotionally, and you should exhaust all other possibilities before taking that route.

MAKING SURE YOUR HEALTH INSURANCE COVERAGE WORKS FOR YOU
How to get your claims paid

I am in the insurance business and have had my fair share of frustrations in dealing with insurance companies. To help get your claims paid in a timely fashion, your first step is to make sure you understand what is covered by your policy and what isn't covered. Read your handbook, check with your human resource department if you work for a company, or call the toll-free number on the back of your insurance card for an explanation of anything that is unclear.

It is critical to find out when you need prior authorization or approval for any procedures or therapies and to carefully follow whatever protocols your insurance company requires. If you want to use an out-of-network doctor, call in advance to see how much it will cost and then find out what your insurance company will pay so you know what to expect. Take lots of notes whenever speaking with insurance company representatives and doctors' offices.

Be persistent when following up on claims. If you end up having a disagreement with your insurance company, you have a few options. To find out how to dispute a claim in your state, you can go to kff.org/ConsumerGuide. You can also get free assistance at PatientAdvocate.org. At HealthProponent.com you can sign up for a paid service to help you with your claims, or ask your employer to consider signing up for HealthAdvocate.com to provide advocacy services to all employees in your company.

SUMMARY

Do the research and figure out what needs to be done to get the best possible services for your child.

Do not be afraid to seek help from others. There are many people who will be glad to assist you.

Get out there, stand tall, and fight for your child's rights. You and your child will never regret it.

8
TAKING
SMALL
STEPS

OVERVIEW

The lessons in this book were learned over many years.

Don't feel overwhelmed. You can accomplish what has been outlined.

Be patient, take things slowly, and acknowledge your progress.

You will make strides if you stay focused on doing what's best for you and your family to help you survive and thrive.

CONGRATULATIONS
You have taken an important step

If you have gotten this far, congratulations, you are well on your way towards not only surviving but thriving in caring for your child with special needs.

There are many suggestions and strategies in this handbook and it will take time for you to make progress even in any one area. Do not try to do everything at once; otherwise you will be overwhelmed and will feel discouraged.

SET A FEW SMALL GOALS
Take it slowly

It took my family years to get where we are today. We are still learning, still making mistakes, and there are always setbacks and difficult times, but we are constantly working to make things better. Start by setting a few small goals and then figure out what actions you need to take to get you there. Talk to other parents who have children with special needs and find out some of the things that have worked for them. Always think about who can help you to achieve your goals.

BE PATIENT
It takes time

Be patient, acknowledge your progress, and be confident that you will achieve your goals, because you will. Periodically review your achievements because it will make you feel better knowing that you are moving forward.

Small incremental changes add up to major improvements. Down the road when you look back to where you started, you will feel a great deal of pride and satisfaction as you see the fruits of your labor.

SUMMARY

It will take time, effort and patience to achieve
your goals.

Good luck and keep on working at it.

In the end, you and your family will be happy you did.

APPENDIX

YOUR CHILD HANDBOOK

Create a binder containing everything there is to know about your child, including medical history, school information, and all related correspondence and evaluations. It will serve as a handy reference guide for you, for new doctors or therapists, and for anyone who might care for your child while you are away or if something happens to you. Update the binder at least once a year, keep it somewhere that is easily accessible, and let other people know where it is.

Below is a list of items to include. Use tabbed sections or dividers to make it easy to find everything. Download blank forms at Drive4Rebecca.org.

DAILY SCHEDULE

> School schedule and directions
>
> After–school/extracurricular activities information, contact people, and directions
>
> Medications
>
> Therapies

EDUCATION/SCHOOL INFORMATION

> Copy of most current IEP and all related correspondence and evaluations
>
> School information — names of teachers, therapists, other staff and contact information

LEGAL

> Any legal documents including wills and trust documents
>
> Contact information of estate planning and special education attorneys/advocates

MEDICAL

Ask for and keep copies of all medical records and x-rays

Complete list of doctors and contact information, notes about each doctor, your experience with them and how they helped (or didn't help)

Medications, including doses and any special instructions

Allergies

Special diets

Therapies/therapists — contact information and any special notes and directions

Behavioral information — to explain some of the specifics about your child

HEALTH INSURANCE

Policy number, group number and telephone number

Copy of insurance card

Additional insurance-related information, including how to submit claims and sample claim forms

PUBLIC BENEFITS/DIVISION OF DEVELOPMENTAL DISABILITY INFORMATION

Information on government agencies that provide various services, including respite programs

Early intervention program details and contact information

EMERGENCY CONTACTS

Names and contact information of friends and family members

BABYSITTERS

Contact information and any special instructions for babysitters

THE MAKE ME FEEL GOOD PLANNER™

You only have so much time each day and you should spend it with people who you enjoy. Life gets stressful and the last thing you need is to be with people who bring you down. Use *The Make Me Feel Good Planner* to list all of the people you would like to spend more time with in your life. Aim to only spend time with people that make you feel either good or great, who are nice to your kids and make you laugh and smile (for relatives, friends and business associates).

1) List all the people you spend time with, and the people you don't spend much time with but would like to see more often, that make you feel either Good, Great or just Okay.

2) Write down the next steps for everyone on your list: Make plans, Call to say hello, etc.

3) Scan your list, start making plans with the Greats and Goods, and save the Okays for last. Periodically you will hear from or run into people who truly make you feel awful. When that happens, make small talk, be polite, but never initiate plans. If they say "let's get together", say let's do that one of these days — and just leave it at that.

4) Redo your list every so often to make sure you keep seeing the people you want to see.

Here are some examples:

Name Friend, Family, Business	How they make me feel Good, Great, Okay	Next step Action
Susan Smith	Great	Call for lunch
Jill Adams	Okay	Call or email
Sandy and Mark Jones	Good	Make plans w/kids
Bill Rogers	Okay	Call to say hi
Tony Samuels	Great	Call for movie or dinner
Joe Taylor	Good	Catch up

THE MAKE ME FEEL GOOD PLANNER™

Name Friend, Family, Business	How they make me feel Good, Great, Okay	Next step Action

YOUR FAMILY ACHIEVEMENT DIARY™

Use *Your Family Achievement Diary* to record what your children accomplish each day, at home and in school. If they are unable to tell you about their school day, ask their teachers to send home notes to fill you in.

At the end of the week, or whenever you need something to pick you up, read the entries in your diary and it will make you smile. Take every opportunity to acknowledge and celebrate their progress by letting them know how proud you are of even their smallest achievements every day.

Use your notes in the Further Progress column to create an action plan of new goals to be accomplished and use this diary for all of your children. As time goes on and you look back at everything, you will be astounded at all of their achievements.

Here are some examples:

Achievement	Why Important	Further Progress
45 minutes at the diner with Rebecca and she was great	Great for us to be able to go out together	Try somewhere new next time
Sam did great in track	He's running faster and having fun	Help him make better food choices so he'll have more energy and do even better
Rebecca did great with delivering items at school	It's a great new skill	Keep getting better at it and introduce new items

YOUR FAMILY ACHIEVEMENT DIARY™

Achievement	Why Important	Further Progress

YOUR GRATITUDE DIARY™

Use *Your Gratitude Diary* to record what you appreciate each day about friends, family, and the world around you.

Studies conducted by Robert A. Emmons, of the University of California, Davis and Michael E. McCullough of the University of Miami show that people who kept gratitude journals were happier, healthier and more optimistic compared with a control group that did not keep a journal. Martin Seligman of the University of Pennsylvania recommends visiting someone to read what you wrote about them as part of a gratitude visit to make the impact on you and others even more powerful.

Use your notes in the Further Progress column to create an action plan of how to show your gratitude.

At the end of the week, or whenever you need something to pick you up, read the entries in your diary and it will make you smile.

Here are some examples:

What I am grateful for	Why Important	Further Progress
My kids	They are terrific	I have to tell them more often
A walk today in a beautiful nature center	It was great to be out enjoying nature	I will schedule time to go monthly
My wife is a great cook	We're so lucky to get such amazing dinners	We need to show our appreciation every day

YOUR GRATITUDE DIARY™

What I am grateful for	Why Important	Further Progress

GENERAL INFORMATION FOR HIRING BABYSITTERS

SAMPLE BABYSITTER ADVERTISEMENT

Help Wanted – Childcare – Your Town – Great Kids! 4 & 7 yr. old.
Refs & Sim. Exp. Req'd. 30–40 Hrs/wk (2:30–8:30) & Read/Write
Eng., Car, N/Smkg Home 201 555–1212

USING VOICEMAIL

We set up a voice mailbox and did not give out our home number. We found that it was better to listen to messages and then decide which candidates we wanted to call back. We generally did best with people who left detailed messages.

SAMPLE VOICEMAIL MESSAGE

Hello. Thank you for calling about our childcare position.
Please leave a very detailed message with your name, telephone
number, the best time to reach you, and tell us why you think
you are the best person for the job. Thank you.

INTERVIEWING

- Prescreen candidates on the phone before interviewing in person

- Always interview with another person (spouse, significant other, friend)

- Take good notes

- Be repetitive; people lie

- Tell everything there is to know about your child

TELEPHONE INTERVIEW QUESTIONS

Introduce yourself and ask, "Do you have a few minutes to talk about the position?"

1. Tell me about your past babysitting jobs? How many kids did
you take care of, what were their ages, how long did you
work with them?

2. Why are you looking for a job?

3. How many hours do you want to work (or are you available to work ___ hours a week)?

4. Have you ever taken care of a child with special needs? Please explain

5. Where do you live?

6. Do you drive and have your own car?

7. Did you go to school? What did you study? Have you taken CPR?

8. Do you smoke? Are you in good health? Do you have any back problems?

9. What are you looking to earn?

10. Do you have health insurance? We require that you have health insurance.

IN-PERSON INTERVIEW QUESTIONS

Ask again about their experience:

1. Why do you want to be a babysitter?

2. What do you see as the perfect babysitter job?

3. What kind of things do you like to do with infants, with toddlers and then with older children? Have you ever cared for a child with special needs?

4. What do you do if a child is misbehaving?

5. Have you ever had to deal with an emergency situation?

6. What do you like to do in your free time? Any hobbies or interests?

7. What is your educational background?

8. Are you in good health?

9. Have you had or are you willing to take CPR and baby first aid training?

10. Do you have any questions for us?

QUESTIONS FOR REFERENCES

(Never interview candidates who cannot provide 2 or 3 references that are not relatives)

1. How do you know (babysitter) or how did you find him or her?

2. Why isn't (babysitter) working for you anymore?

3. What about (babysitter) was not the greatest, or was there anything that bothered you, even something small that was just annoying?

4. Did you leave (babysitter) alone with your children? My child has special needs (say if your child does not speak) and it is critical to know that they will be safe and well cared for because they may not be able to tell us.

5. How flexible was (babysitter)? (People who are married or have kids are generally less flexible.)

6. How did (babysitter) get to work? Did (babysitter) drive your kids? (Having a car gives them more flexibility.)

7. Was (babysitter) always on time?

8. Was (babysitter) available for special situations when they weren't scheduled?

9. How did (babysitter) communicate? Was (babysitter) good at listening?

10. Did (babysitter) do cleaning and, was it light or heavy cleaning, and did he/she do a good job?

11. Is (babysitter) in good health? Could (babysitter) run along side a child riding a bicycle with training wheels?

SENSITIVITY EXERCISES FOR INCLUSION

We were given the following advice from the director of inclusion from The JCC of Greater Washington before our daughter started as a Girl Scout at age five. As she has grown older, we have adapted these exercises for different situations to accommodate the changing interests and levels of understanding of other children.

> "*If there is a parent meeting, that would be the time to tell the parents about Rebecca.*"

You may want to check with the troop leader to get her perspective. Something should certainly be done with the kids in the group. You can decide if you want Rebecca to be there when they talk about her or if you do not. We have done it both ways, depending on the age of the child and his or her needs and comfort level. I'm sure you have experience with this and probably know very good words to use, but the idea would be to be very honest about her differences and then to point out her similarities.

For example, "Rebecca isn't able to speak because the part of her brain that should make her speak is broken, but she does understand what you are saying to her and she loves Power Puff Girls (or whatever 5 year old girls in New Jersey are into!!)." I'm not sure that exactly describes Rebecca, but it is an example of the kind of language I have used with 5 year olds.

I think you do want to have some type of communication with the other parents so that they do not feel that something is being hidden from them. I think that is where fear and prejudice comes from.

I think the key to sensitivity exercises with 5 year olds is to keep it very simple. One thing I have done is a game of "charades." Ask them to give someone a message without speaking. Give them very specific directions, i.e. "How can you tell Susie that you want to be her friend without speaking?" or "Show that you are excited about being in the Daisies" (again without speaking). It may be difficult to simulate Rebecca's disability in a meaningful way to five year olds, but you can simulate other disabilities which helps to eliminate some fear and mystery about disabilities in general. Simple things like being blindfolded and having a friend lead them around the room works well.

You could teach them the ASL sign language alphabet. The important piece is to talk about each activity after they do it. When I do activities such as "charades," I explain that kids who are not able to speak still want and need to communicate and to participate in everything. There is a great T-shirt that says, "Not being able to speak is not the same as not having anything to say." That may be lost on 5 year olds, but that is the concept I try to get across. When I worked with first graders last year I showed them a Braille version of Seventeen magazine. Those kinds of things help to show them that people with disabilities are interested in the same things that they are interested in."

SENSITIVITY EXERCISES FOR INCLUSION SCRIPT

These are examples of exercises you can do with children with whom your child will interact. The idea is to be to be very honest about differences between your child and them, and to point out similarities.

You can say, "_____ can't speak because the part of her brain that should make her speak is broken. But she understands a lot of things that you say to her."
The kids may ask questions at this point; for example, "If her brain is broken, why don't you take her to the hospital or a doctor to get it fixed?"
    You can say "_____ goes to doctors who are helping her, and in school her teachers also help her in many ways."

Ask, "Who likes peanut butter and jelly? And who likes pizza"
    Some or all of the kids will raise their hands.
    Say, "_____loves peanut butter and jelly and pizza too."
    Ask who likes swimming… skating… skiing … bike riding?
    Say _____ loves all those things too, and she is also a Girl Scout.

Ask, "Who has a brother or sister?" Again, some or all of the kids will raise their hands.
    Say, "_____has a little brother named _____ and two dogs."
    You can then show them pictures of _____ and her family.

Tell them that you are going to play a game — Ask them to give someone a message without speaking (and give them very specific directions).
    Say, "How can you tell Sarah that you want to be her friend without speaking?" You will need to ask for two volunteers. The kids might hug, smile at each other, hold hands, etc.
    Say, "Show that you are excited about being here, again without speaking."
    Ask for two different volunteers again. They might clap or jump up and down.
    Explain that "kids who are not able to speak still want and need to communicate and to be with everyone." Say, "_____ sometimes waves her arms around when she is happy, or makes different types of sounds, and sometimes she cries when she is sad or scared, and she smiles and laughs when she is happy. And she loves hugs, and to be around other kids like all of you. She can't speak, but she understands a lot, and just like you she likes when people are nice to her."

COMMUNITY SERVICE ASSISTANCE
SAMPLE LETTER

Dear Mrs. _____:

Thank you for taking the time to describe some of the wonderful community service efforts supported by your school, and for letting your terrific students know about the opportunity to work with Rebecca. Any assistance would be a great help to her and to our family.

We are in constant need of help and companionship for Rebecca, and we have hired various babysitters over the years to assist us (we could truly use help seven days a week).

Since we have a limited budget to hire babysitters, we are very appreciative of the generosity of any students willing to volunteer as part of community service and to become a part of our lives.

It might help to show a picture of Rebecca to your students, to help them make a connection with her. We have enclosed a few pictures and a flyer to post for your students.

Thank you again for your help.

Sincerely,
Michey and Jon

SAMPLE FLYER

To the Terrific Teenagers of [school name]

Our sweet six-year-old daughter Rebecca has a rare genetic disorder that causes autistic tendencies. Rebecca does not speak, and does not have a strong ability to communicate, but she participates with assistance in many different types of activities, (swimming, bike riding, roller skating, horseback riding, skiing, etc.). Rebecca is making good progress overall, but needs constant one-on-one assistance.

We were very happy to learn about the [school name] Community Service Program. Thank you for reading the following about Rebecca, and for your interest in working with her in any capacity. Rebecca is very cute and is generally a happy and loving girl. We can always use an extra hand around the house after school, during weekends, and over school holidays (we also have a typical fun-loving three-year-old named Sam).

We try to include Rebecca in everything we do, such as meals at restaurant, family functions, outings to amusement parks, and even just trips to the supermarket; having someone come along to help always makes it easier. Rebecca also participates in a Girl Scout troop, and that is another area where we can always use some help. The more that Rebecca is exposed to different types of situations, and the more familiar those situations become to her, the more success she has.

We welcome you to come by and meet Rebecca, and get a better idea about what it would be like to work with her. We can provide training at our home after school, when teachers, therapists and a few babysitters (who have been like big sisters to her for several years) are with Rebecca.

Thank you so much for your interest. Having more people who are able to work with Rebecca makes our lives much more manageable, allows her to be a more active participant in the community, and can potentially expose more individuals to the opportunity to work with her and other children and families in similar situations. Please call to learn more about Rebecca and our family.

SPECIAL NEEDS RESOURCES

ADVOCACY AND SPECIAL NEEDS INFORMATION

AdvocacyForAll.org

The Arc — TheArc.org
800 433-5255

Autism Speaks Autism Response Team
888-AUTISM2

Autism Society of America
AutismSource.org
800-3AUTISM

Council of Parent and Attorney Advocates
COPAA.org

Drive4Rebecca.org Resource page
(state by state directory)

Guide for Health Insurance Disputes
KFF.org/ConsumerGuide
650 854-9400

HealthAdvocate.com
610 825-1222

HealthProponent.com
866 939-3435

National Association of Healthcare Advocates
NAHAC.com

National Organization on Disability
NOD.org
202 293-5960

PatientAdvocate.org
800 532-5274

ESTATE PLANNING

Academy of Special Needs Planners
SpecialNeedsAnswers.com
866 296-5509

The Special Needs Alliance
SpecialNeedsAlliance.org
877 572-8472

FINANCIAL PLANNING

Mass Mutual SpecialCare program
800 272-2216
MassMutual.com

Merrill Lynch Special Needs Financial Services
TotalMerrill.com
877 456-7526

MetLife Center for Special Needs Planning
MetLife.com
877 638-3375

INCLUSION INFORMATION

Inclusion.com

InclusionForAll.org
Focused on summer camp inclusion

Kids Included Together
KITonline.org
858 225-5680

SPORTS PROGRAMS

Adaptive Sports Programs Worldwide
sitski.com/pg3.htm   *continued*

SPORTS PROGRAMS *continued*

American Special Hockey Association
AmericanSpecialHockey.org

Special Olympics
SpecialOlympics.org
800 700-8585

OTHER RESOURCES

Association for Behavior Analysis
ABAInternational.org
269 492-9310

Care.com
Web site for finding caregivers

Lekotek.org
Toys for kids with special needs
773 528-5766

Nannies4Hire.com
Web site for finding caregivers
402 379-4121

National Down Syndrome Society
NDDS.org
800 221-4602

National Family Caregivers Association
nfcacares.org
800 896-3650

Nolo.com
Download WillMaker to create a basic will until you
have a chance to meet with an estate planning attorney
800 728-3555

United Cerebral Palsy
UCP.org
800 872-5827

ABOUT THE AUTHOR

Rebecca and Jon Singer

Jon Singer would do just about anything for his kids, and especially to make sure his daughter, Rebecca, who has a rare genetic disorder that causes autistic tendencies, gets what she needs to succeed. He'd practically go to the end of the earth if that's what it would take.

In fact, that's just what he did. In the summer of 2002, Jon and his wife, Michey formed an organization called The Drive for Rebecca (Drive4Rebecca. org) to increase awareness of autism and raise desperately needed funds for autism research and education. To raise money for the new organization, Jon and Michey, together with Rebecca; her brother, Sam; their cousin, Evan; and their babysitter, Rachel set out on a cross-country journey that changed their lives.

They drove from New Jersey to Los Angeles in a decorated motor home, staying in hotel rooms that were generously provided free of charge by a leading hotel chain. They organized events at Whole Foods Market and Wild Oats stores in seven cities, with sponsors such as Build-A-Bear Workshop, drawing media coverage from all the major networks. Along the journey they were greeted by friends, family members, Girl Scouts and made many new acquaintances.

They raised nearly $100,000, which they donated to autism research projects and to leading educational programs for kids with autism that use the science of Applied Behavioral Analysis. They ultimately joined forces with five other New Jersey families to start an incredible new school called REED Academy (REEDAcademy.org), where Rebecca could learn and grow to the best of her abilities, and donated funds to support the opening of another school.

Rebecca and twenty other students have been making amazing progress since REED Academy opened in 2003. Because of the miracles that happen every day at REED, several students have graduated and are attending their local elementary schools together with typically developing peers.

RAVE REVIEWS FROM AROUND THE WORLD

"Congratulations on The Special Needs Parent Handbook. It looks like it will be a valuable life-line to many parents in the same or similar situation. Your writing is candid and clear, humorous and realistic."

– Keren, USA

"This was EXTREMELY helpful to me. I have a special needs child myself and I have been trying to get some ideas on how to include him in activities with other children."

– Bonnie, Canada

"I recently read Jonathan Singer's book and it was a refreshing and uplifting piece that was not the typical financial guide for parents with a special needs child. He addresses the most difficult issues with a special light-hearted flair — an informal, easy to read how-to-book. This book will empower parents to make the practical decisions necessary to provide the optimal upbringing for their special needs child and at the same time develop a deep relationship with their spouse and make it inclusive and special for the other children."

– David Halper CLU/CHFC and partner
Halper Rawiszer Financial Group, USA

"Thank you for your encouraging words. They were just what I needed to hear today. God bless."

– Claudia, NZ

"This information was very helpful thank you so much. I am a young single parent of 2 and my youngest has downs and its been hard."

– Miranda, USA

"I especially liked the strategies for keeping the family together."

– Taya, Canada

"I am a doctor in the UK working in primary care. From time to time I have a look around the web to see if there is anything that would be beneficial to the children I see. I thought that it was a really wonderful account .... I really liked your friendly, readable style, and I am sure that other parents would find your comments helpful."

– Dr. Gill, UK

"Keeping the Family Together was very interesting. I was wondering if I could put it in a newsletter I send out to parents who are raising children with special needs."

– Cheryl, USA

"Thank you so much ... Our marriage is really feeling the strain at times and this article has helped a lot."

– Jo, UK

"Very enlightening. Stumbled on to your website accidentally, whilst searching for info on the disabled in the workplace."

– Florence, South Africa

"Great book — would love to be able to use this as part of the work I do with social care students in Ireland to understand the needs of families with special needs children. Keep up the good work!"

– Jennifer, Ireland

"Thank you for writing the Special Needs Handbook. In Chapter One, 'Keeping the Family together,' it is evident the author lives this journey everyday, has done his research, and uses all this experience, wisdom from various sources and data for supporting special needs families — a first things first approach to supporting special needs children.

With this book, a parent who is on the special needs journey gets a buddy to help add perspective — like a tourist guide. This tourist guide is holistic and honest, a gem in 'Holland' — and so essential to healthy progress for everyone in the family. Many perspectives for keeping a good attitude and uplifted spirits are in the book, but always with an honest look at reality and acceptance of the feelings everyone's too afraid to speak of — for fear of judgement, isolation and rejection from society at large. Get the book — get relief — get an honest guide to 'Holland'."

– Deborah, USA

"Hi, Jonathan. I found this excerpt at Pediatric Minds, www.pediatricminds. com. This has been really helpful as we are learning how to parent two special needs children. I have started an email support group and yahoo group for parents of gifted and special needs children, and I have forwarded this excerpt to the groups."

– Marcie, USA

"I think your book is amazing. I have worked with special students for 19 years and only once did I encounter any in servicing relating to family. I don't think anyone other than parents like yourselves know the commitment and lack of help available to parents like yourselves. I will recommend we purchase a copy of your book for the Unit in which I presently work. Good luck."

– Robyn, Australia

"Every family who has a Child with a Disability needs one of these."

Kind regards,

– Bronwyn, Australia
Administration Officer, Department of Communities,
Disability Community Care Services
Far Northern Queensland Region

"What a Resource!

I've only read the intro but it reminded me that it is more than ok to keep advocating for our special need daughters, even in the areas such as health and education where sometimes as parents we think these systems might have the expertise."

– Thank you
Jo, Australia

"GREAT BOOK (so far). I am glad you wrote this book and look forward to finishing it. I just read the beginning and LOVED the Holland/Italy analogy. I read that to my older two kids and they liked it too. They said they wouldn't trade their brothers but they "wish they were more Italian," which has a double meaning since the girls are half Italian but the boys are half Russian (different Dads). LOL!

And I am glad you mentioned single moms a little too. Its nice to see a mention about our struggles. Its not easy when one parent decides they can't handle the stress and bails out on the family-and its even worse when its because you have kids with "issues." A lot of people tell me they just can't imagine dealing with my life and I tell them all its not up to me to decide when my plate is full, its up to God. :) Although I do pray a lot for some free space on that plate.

Good luck on all that you are doing, God bless you all, and keep up the fight!!!"

– Sam, USA

"I LIKED THE ENTIRE BOOK.....REALLY! As the parent of a son with autism, I did a lot of your suggestions, just as common sense and a positive attitude. BUT, it is hard for many families to do that and sometimes hard for me. I'm so glad this book is out. Even though my son is 17, I would still like to read it, especially the part about keeping the family together. This could be very helpful because we have a typical, advanced, gifted 10-year old son.

The vacation information is especially helpful, more so now that my husband is laid off. We all need a vacation, no matter how short. THANK YOU FOR WRITING THIS BOOK. I wish it would have been written sooner, but I'm glad it is now out."

– Lenore, USA

"I really enjoyed reading the excerpt "How To Keep the Family Together" I loved all the things that your family did and do to keep your family together. My family does not have those resources, but maybe one day we will. It was very encouraging to read. I loved reading it!"

– Jennifer, USA

"I read your book excerpts and they are good. The tone is positive but not fluff. I appreciate it because life is hard not fluffy.

I have always been a single mom but I applaud that you have learned how to hold your relationship and family together. That is great!

My 9 year old son is on the spectrum. We have been through so much. I am an advocate for my son. I have educated myself on insurance, IEP, laws and health issues. I love my son more than life itself, and because of this I have become a force to be reckoned with.

May God bless and keep all of you."

– Kind Regards,
Deanna, USA

"From what I've seen so far, this looks like a great book to have. Can't wait to see the whole book!

Thanks for your great work, it will help not only my family but many, many more."

– Liz, USA

"THANK YOU!!! I really appreciate reading about other parents who are where I am (and can't wait to read every word of the book when it come out). It is a comfort to hear stories of other parents who found themselves unexpectedly landing in 'Holland.' This morning, in fact, was one of those mornings, medically, and I needed an arm on my shoulder... thank you for providing that with the excerpt."

– Rhea, USA

"I love the book! Very motivating and inspirational yet practical. There is something in there for everyone. My favorite chapter is about "Keeping the Family Together." At times, we are so close as a family unit but the unknown can often cause strain. We need more references/books that really put things into perspective. We often are too quick to judge or set lower expectations for our children with special needs, when in fact the truth of the matter is...the higher the goal you set the more they will achieve. My son is constantly exceeding my expectations. A book like this continues to remind me just how lucky I am. Thank you for writing it!"

– Rosemarie, USA

"I love what you are doing with your kids. The comparison of Italy and Holland is right on. Keep sending out these positive vibes and sharing with families still struggling day by day. I look forward to hearing more as I read the rest of your book."

– DR, USA

"I loved the excerpt especially the part with the poem, Welcome to Holland. It reminds me of how wonderful my son is even if he is not Italy, No especially because he is not Italy. Everyone else is Italy but he is a priceless and rare treasure."

– Alina, USA

"I am completely in awe of families and parents like you. It is such an overwhelming and daunting task to raise a child with special needs. My son has autism and at this very point I am overwhelmed again trying to figure out a summer plan for him. Every year we get to this place of searching the internet and filling out applications for aid to go to specialized camps (which are much more expensive than regular camps).

I was pleasantly surprised at the realistic approach that you have taken with your book and the analogy about a trip to Holland. That is so true. I love my child with everything that is in me however I still have those weepy days wondering if he will ever have friends. I was uplifted to see your positive approach to figuring this whole thing out because I don't believe that anyone is fully prepared for all of the responsibilities involved. Because our diagnoses is Autism we are participating in biomedical treatment in addition to therapy and managing that requires another skill set.

From the excepts that I have read, I think the book is great for people that do not have to be caregivers of special needs as well as those that are. The stories are interesting and easy to follow, it is not clinical nor intimidating. I think that different audiences will find it helpful and useful.

Keep up the outstanding work."

– Kim, USA

"Wow, I have to say that what I have read so far, I liked! I want to read more!!!!

The one thing that I have found, and I believe you found…the secret of thriving as a family with special needs children, is…accept and even embrace the special need. Make it a 'normal' part of your life. If you fight against it, you give it power, it can control you. If you embrace it, make it a part of your life and work with it (not against it) you then control it, it does not control you. Go out to the zoo with a contingency plan in place. In our home NOTHING is set in stone. We live a very fluid life. I feel so bad for those who have always lived on a schedule, walking the straight and narrow…they are the ones that struggle with a special family, wandering outside the line is our norm, we just stop and smell the flowers along the way. It sounds like you do too.

Can't wait to read what else you have to say."

– Jeannie, USA

"I just read an excerpt from you book. It was the chapter on taking special needs kids out in public. I think you did a good job with it. I like that you talk about not really caring about what others think and concentrating on your daughter's needs. I also love the part about enlisting other kids help. I have two kids with autism and going out in public can definitely be a challenge and it is most definitely never dull. LOL. Enlisting the help of other kids is an amazing strategy. Most people are thrilled to be given a way to help someone with special needs, and when they do they become that person's advocate.

I am so glad you've written this book. When my kids were younger, I wanted answers about how to navigate the world with my kids. I could never find a resource that gave practical advice and real world examples. Your book seems to do just that, and will be a real lifesaver to parents new to the world of special needs. I think us veterans will benefit as well."

– Janice, USA

"I enjoyed what I read and feel it will help others work with students with special needs. Good luck with this project!"

– Christopher, USA
Counselor, Thaddeus Stevens College of Technology

"Wow! I am so excited to read more. My daughter is 10 year old named Rebecca and they sound so similar. I am forming a family to family network in my area and desperately need your advice. This is great timing for us. Thank you for investing your time to improve lives of children like ours."

– Kim, USA

"What I read was very informational and looks like a great resource for families with kids with special needs. I read the portion that talked about hiring a babysitter or help. Thanks so much for putting this book together and I am so glad that someone is working with advocacy and support for families with kids with special needs."

– Rebecca, USA

"Awesome reading. Wish this had been available 3 years ago when I was really struggling. I like your writing style, down to earth, easy to read, realistic as can be, and the humor is great. Just what we need to make it through another day. Thanks, great book."

– Patti, USA

"Thank you for this resource-great for new families to autism and ones on down the road in their journey."

– Sherry, USA

"I just finished reading some of your excerpts and I am very impressed with your book. As a Mom of two children on the spectrum, along with two neuro typical children, I can relate to everything you have written. SO much so that along with how you have made a commitment to your life to help others. Congratulations!"

– Kathy, USA

"I think the tips and strategies in this book will be excellent to try with my own daughter!"

– Diane, USA

"This book has some good tips. Keep up the excellent work."

– Suzanne, USA

"I wanted to let you know that I think your handbook is invaluable to parents who have children with special needs as well as teachers."

– Carolyn, USA

"The Special Needs Parent Handbook is a well-written, down-to-earth guidebook that reads like a conversation with a good friend. Singer offers tips for interacting with a child with special needs that he has learned through his first-hand experience of raising both a child with special needs as well as one without."

– Harry S. Margolis
Academy of Special Needs Planners, USA

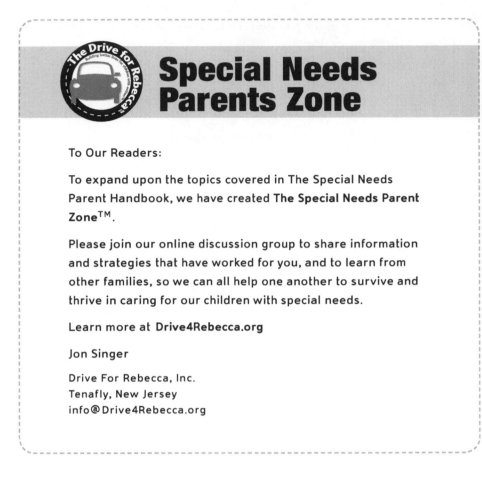

Special Needs Parents Zone

To Our Readers:

To expand upon the topics covered in The Special Needs Parent Handbook, we have created **The Special Needs Parent Zone**™.

Please join our online discussion group to share information and strategies that have worked for you, and to learn from other families, so we can all help one another to survive and thrive in caring for our children with special needs.

Learn more at **Drive4Rebecca.org**

Jon Singer

Drive For Rebecca, Inc.
Tenafly, New Jersey
info@Drive4Rebecca.org

WHAT DID YOU THINK ABOUT THE BOOK?

Did you love it, hate it, can't live without it?

We would appreciate your feedback.

Please email us at info@Drive4Rebecca.org so we can make future editions even better and add more helpful information online.

If you really liked the book, thank you for adding a review on Amazon.com.

Enjoy a sample chapter
from Jon Singer's
upcoming book *Driven*.

DrivenStory.com

Driven is a project on Kickstarter.
Backers of *Driven* can enjoy:

A VIP lunch at Nobu NY, the flagship restaurant of Chef Nobu Matsuhisa, partner of restaurateur Drew Nieporent and Oscar-winning actor Robert De Niro.

Get on THE RIDE, a super-sized, technologically amped up vehicle that travels the streets of New York with stadium-style, sideways seating and massive windows, followed by a fireside chat (brick oven fire that is) about the book at the world famous John's Pizza in Times Square.

An exclusive NYC book launch party in the fall at a cool NYC location (to be announced) ... and more.

Get the whole story about Driven on:
www.DrivenStory.com

Thanks,
Jon "Driven" Singer

Driven : A father's relentless crusade to help his daughter and help change the world.

Disclaimer - All characters appearing in this work are real. Any resemblance to real persons, living or dead, is purely intentional. The actions of individuals named in this book should not reflect upon or be an indictment of the institutions they are or have been affiliated with in the past.

The views expressed in this book are those of the author and do not represent the views of his wife or children and should not be held against them.

It's all Jon's fault. Period.

ABOUT DRIVEN

In 1997 a young couple was told that their beautiful baby girl was one of 30 individuals around the globe having a rare genetic disorder with no name. **Although little was known about this condition at the time, the doctor said "if you have any hopes of her having similar intelligence to either of you, it is doubtful, and she may never walk."** Imagine the impact that this cruel and callous statement could have had on these emotionally fragile parents, and how it might have killed whatever hopes and dreams they had for the future.

And imagine how many other families since that time had their hopes and dreams crushed by that doctor (I will refer to her as Dr. W.), and other insensitive doctors. Think of the lost potential of so many children whose parents may simply have given up upon hearing such news because they were convinced that their efforts would be futile.

That sweet little girl was our daughter Rebecca, and fortunately for her, that experience only served as my challenge to prove Dr. W. wrong. Today, with some assistance, Rebecca roller blades, skis, rides horses and a bicycle, and sometimes breaks out into a little jog. And ironically, almost 14 years later to the day, in the same hospital where we heard those incredibly painful words, there was new found hope for Rebecca in an exciting clinical trial that recently began. At the time, we were told we needed to have a genetic workup done by Dr. W. Rather than having a highly charged confrontation, we refused to meet and they arranged for us to see another geneticist instead.

For you doctors who would like to learn something from this experience, what

Dr. W. could have said differently was something along these lines - "I have done some research and have discovered there are only 30 cases of what Rebecca has in the entire world. Unfortunately, while there are too few cases to really know the long term prospects, from what we have seen so far these individuals are significantly affected by this disorder. Perhaps things will be different for your daughter but we really just don't know. We hope and pray for the best for you and for her."

Years ago we learned from Drs. Arnold and Sandra Gold, founders of the Gold Foundation for Humanism in Medicine, that the best doctors are not necessarily the ones that win all the awards or nominations in magazines or other reports. While the best doctors are highly qualified and have achieved excellence in their chosen field, their level of skill must be matched by their level of humanity and kindness. I will always choose the doctor with the second or third best reputation for excellence in their particular area of speciality if they are known to have the best bedside manner. No one deserves to be treated poorly by a medical professional and especially not parents of children with special needs.

Finally, in these exciting times, with all of the advances in medical technology and the study of genetics, doctors must choose their words carefully and not pretend to have a crystal ball. You never know what may happen, every child is different, and never ever discount the power and passion of a driven parent.

WHY DRIVEN

In Driven, I will share my life lessons that can be applied to overcome practically any obstacle, transforming problems into challenges to be solved. While many of the stories in this book are about situations involving my daughter, the results have often benefitted many other children and families and our experiences can be instructive and the lessons applied to many different types of situations.

Words used to describe me by various people in my life have included "resourceful," "creative," "politely persistent" and "incredibly impatient" (some of my friends and family members would probably add "annoying" to this short list and Michey is convinced I am crazy.) My greatest achievements over the years have come about when I have been able to apply these capabilities all at once (and a little crazy probably has been helpful too!)

I was asked what I meant in the subtitle by "help to change the world." I have learned over the years that the more optimism you have, the more you challenge the status quo, and the more you fight for what you believe in, the more you can and will change the world in many different ways. My friend and mentor Dan

Sullivan, founder of The Strategic Coach Program, has always stressed the importance of teamwork and doing something bigger than yourself. By following Dan's advice, and by applying some or all of the the factors mentioned above, it can make a huge impact on others, be inspirational, and help make the world a better place to live.

HOW I BECAME DRIVEN

If 20 years ago a fortune teller told me "one day you and your wife are going to have a daughter with significant special needs, establish a foundation to help her and many other children and families, raise over $1,000,000, help open a new school, drive across the country, twice, holding fundraising events in several cities, and write three books sharing your experiences" I would have said "I'm not having kids".

I joke but, back then, my wife Michey and I never could have imagined the life long journey we would begin after learning that Rebecca had this extremely rare genetic disorder, later called Phelan-McDermid Syndrome, that caused severe developmental delays. We embarked on an adventure that would change our lives forever, touching and inspiring countless others along the way, and we never turned back.

A few years before Rebecca was born, Michey was a rising star in the world of New York City fundraising, planning sometimes extravagant special events for the Museum of Natural History and The American Heart Association that were attended by New York's financial and social elite. Meanwhile, I was selling insurance and helping to grow a family business along with my brother, my sister and our very entrepreneurial dad.

Little did we know how incredibly valuable Michey's skills would prove to become one day when she would assume a leadership role in planning fundraising events for the school we were to help establish called REED Academy.

While I was never particularly charitable, anyone living on the Upper West Side of Manhattan could not help but notice the many homeless people in the neighborhood.

I was particularly struck by the few regulars who reminded me of the inscription on the James Farley Post Office in New York City, "Neither snow nor rain nor heat nor gloom of night stays these couriers from the swift completion of their appointed rounds." Many of these individuals were always there even in the bitter cold.

I always felt accepting something to eat when no money was offered was what separated the "men from the boys", or the people who were really hungry from those that simply wanted money for drugs or alcohol. To illustrate the point, one night, when leaving a supermarket with my brother near Stuyvesant Town, we saw someone waiting just outside of the entrance asking for money. I handed him an apple and moments later, while walking away from the store, the apple came rolling by.

Instead of giving money to homeless people, I began offering to buy them something to eat and typically my offers were eagerly accepted. I also started bringing our leftovers from restaurants to hungry people on the street. The unfortunate prevalence of people struggling to survive in New York City inspired my first charitable initiative called Take Out for the Homeless.

I created a program to encourage restaurant patrons to wrap up their leftovers or order something extra to go to bring to a homeless person waiting outside. I was interviewed on a PBS television station and a number of restaurants agreed to post notices to promote the idea. Take Out for the Homeless was short lived however because soon after the idea was conceived, my attention shifted to focus on our long and painful effort to have children and start a family.

Rebecca made it clear very early on that anything that had to do with her wasn't going to be easy. After two miscarriages, and with the advice of a fertility doctor, Michey ended her fundraising career to reduce stress and help increase the odds of having a successful pregnancy. We even started exploring adoption as an alternative.

After learning that adoption laws were more favorable at the time in New Jersey than they were in New York, we moved to New Jersey. . Soon after we moved, and before we had started looking into adoption, Michey became pregnant with Rebecca.

Rebecca was a beautiful baby but after several months it became apparent that something was wrong. She did not seem to be developing the way she was supposed to. After many visits to New York City specialists, Rebecca was diagnosed with her rare disorder. Our hearts stopped, tears flowed and at that moment our lives changed forever. The doctors said she would be significantly challenged for the rest of her life. We had no idea what that would mean, nor did we have any idea of what was to come, and all of the work we had ahead of us, to help Rebecca and to help many other children with special needs.

MIRACLE ON 99TH STREET

Emotionally, February 2012 was one of the most challenging times for our family and unlike anything we have dealt with for quite some time, perhaps since Rebecca was born.

Rebecca has a rare genetic disorder called Phelan McDermid Syndrome and there are only 700 individuals identified worldwide with this disorder. Going back a few years ago, we found out about some exciting research underway at Mount Sinai's Seaver Autism Center in New York. What they discovered was that when mice whose cells were genetically altered to simulate this disorder were given a human growth hormone for two weeks, their cells reverted to normal!

While what happens with mice does not necessarily translate to humans (nine cancers that have been cured in mice have yet to help cure people), it was amazing to find out that someone was paying attention to and cared about something so rare that affected our daughter. Phelan McDermid Syndrome has now been called a genetic based autism disorder and it seems that through these clinical trials they may be able to gain some answers about related disorders and perhaps unlock more clues about "classic autism" to help many more individuals and families.

We brought Rebecca in to see Dr. Alex Kolevzon and his terrific team at Seaver Autism Center for hours of psychological and genetic testing to confirm that Rebecca would qualify for the trial and she did. Fast forward to December 2011 - we found out that Seaver Autism Center had gained approval from the FDA to get started. We were told however that 30 families had visited Mount Sinai to be tested and evaluated but they only had funding to start with 10.

One major issue in our case was that we were in a bit of a race for time. Because the trial involves a growth hormone, IGF-1, and with Rebecca going on 16, there was a requirement that her growth plates had to be open otherwise it could be dangerous for her to take the drug and she might not be able to participate. As of the past summer, when she had twisted her ankle, an X-ray showed that her growth plates were still open so we were confident but still concerned.

We kept our fingers crossed, and at the end of January we received an email from Alex that Rebecca was chosen to participate in the trial. We were very lucky because one of the most important factors in their selection criteria was geography, meaning they would start with individuals living closest to their facility to allow them to participate without disrupting their normal routine (there are families living around the globe who would mortgage their homes without hesitation to get their children into this trial).

Aside from getting REED Academy started, this was probably the most exciting news we had ever had for Rebecca. Although we were not pinning our hopes on a miracle cure, it was remarkable to learn that there might be something that could help our angel of a daughter, the 700 other families, and perhaps many more individuals affected by autism some day.

While we were celebrating with tears of joy, and we gave our family and a few close friends the great news, just hours later we received a second email. Rebecca would have to take a few tests to confirm she was medically able to withstand the trial, and most critically they needed to reconfirm that her growth plates were still open. While we thought we were pretty much in the clear because of the X-rays from the summer, this put a bit of a damper on the big news and we were anxious to get these tests out of the way and proceed.

It was a Friday and we were told we could come in for X-rays early the next week. By Tuesday I was getting very impatient (no surprise) waiting to hear from their radiology department. I asked if we could go to our local Englewood Hospital instead, which was much more convenient and would be quicker and easier for Rebecca.

That night we went for the X-rays and I took a picture with my iPhone and emailed it to Alex. He was surprised at the quality of the photo and said he would email it right away to Dr. Rapaport, who was their consultant on the project and Chief of Pediatric Endocrinology at Mount Sinai.

Two nail biting hours later we received a devastating blow in the form of a phone call from Alex. He said "I'm so sorry to tell you this, but I spoke with Dr. Rapaport and Rebecca's growth plates are closed. Unfortunately she will be unable to participate in the trials. I can't tell you how sorry I am."

You can only imagine how incredibly upsetting this news was to our family, and in particular to Michey, now that our single greatest hope for Rebecca which was on the near horizon, was suddenly ripped away and was now gone forever. We were up all night and Michey was practically inconsolable. The next morning Sam, our 12-year-old son, cried hysterically when he heard the news.

I was incredibly upset and didn't know what to think or even which way was up or down. Once I gathered my thoughts I decided we would see how the trial went with the other participants and, if there were significant changes, we would somehow find a way to obtain the medication independent of the study. I told Michey I would start looking into the potential dangers to Rebecca, so that we could do a risk/reward analysis and determine if it would make sense to pursue this course of action once the results of the trial were known.

Michey didn't want any part of this. She was finished. She said "I don't want to hear about it anymore because emotionally I can't take it. It's over for me now. Do whatever you need to do but don't talk to me about it, and don't talk to Sam about it anymore and give him false hopes. If something good happens as a result of whatever it is that you want to do that's great, but I am getting off this emotional roller coaster right now."

I completely understood and respected her wishes (for at least a few days).

My first instinct was to spring into action which is probably my way of avoiding emotionally difficult situations and coping so I immediately called our brilliant and loving doctor cousins - Steven Kaplan, an emergency room physician, and Craig Title, an orthopedic surgeon, for advice. I wanted to know the dangers to Rebecca of taking IGF-1 and I asked them to look at the X-ray. Both felt that although there was not a lot of growth potential, Rebecca's growth plate appeared to be partially open.

I received the radiologist's report from Englewood indicating that Rebecca's bone age was 14 and I called Alex with this information and told him what my cousins said about the X-ray. He said he would go back to the endocrinologist and ask him to reconsider.

Several hours later I heard back from Alex. He had argued the point about the bone age and the growth potential but the answer was still no. I asked him if we could get a second opinion and he said he would be open to hearing what another doctor had to say.

Steven recommended calling the heads of Pediatric and Adult Endocrinology at New York Presbyterian while at the same time Craig was reaching out to his colleagues to find out more about IGF-1 and for their opinion about Rebecca's growth plates.

Dr. Vogiatzi, Chief of Pediatric Endocrinology called me back that Friday and spent 30 minutes patiently answering all of my questions. She felt that based on the X-rays, and with the short duration of the trial, the use of IGF-1 should be safe and that we could monitor Rebecca for side effects. I asked if she would speak with Alex and she said that her hospital probably would not want her to give an opinion. NY Presbyterian did not have FDA approval and therefore Mount Sinai might not even be able to accept her input. She recommended calling Dr. Harbison at Mount Sinai who was part of another pediatric endocrinology group that specialized in growth problems.

It was now late Friday afternoon and I tried calling and couldn't reach anyone in Dr. Harbison's department. I found her email address and forwarded all of the information but did not expect to hear back from her until after the weekend. I was pleasantly surprised to receive an email from Dr. Harbison within minutes. She wrote "If the reading of Rebecca's bone age was correct, and her bone age was actually 14 years old, she had 2% of her total adult height left to grow at the time of the X-Ray. The average girl grows the final 2% of her height between 14 and 17 years so technically, her bones should not be closed." I sent her the iPhone photo of the X-ray that had been used to make the initial determination and she replied "This is inadequate to read. Whoever reads it will need the original. I would be glad to help if and only if Drs. Kolevzon (Alex the head researcher) and Buxbaum (Director of Seaver Autism Center) request that I do so" and she copied them on her email message.

I was so excited by this development and raced home especially because I was going be late for our plans to go to our synagogue for Friday night services (the timing was good because a little praying couldn't hurt). When Michey asked why I was late I sarcastically replied "I can't answer that question because it is about something you don't want to hear about." She asked me to tell her what was going on, I did, and while she didn't change her opinion of how she felt about every-thing, Sam overheard our conversation and was elated.

I went into Manhattan and dropped off the X-rays the next morning, and first thing on Monday I called Alex. He hadn't heard back from Dr. Harbison so I called her office and got the bad news - she was going to be out on vacation for the next three weeks.

In further discussions with Alex, I finally got to the bottom of one of the main reasons why they were concerned about the question of growth plates and hav-ing Rebecca reinstated into the trial. He explained that if Rebecca had a negative reaction to the drug, they would have to report that to the FDA, and if the FDA found she hadn't met the criteria for the trials, they would shut them down and they were not willing to take that chance.

I asked him to explain exactly what all of that meant. Alex said that there were exclusion criteria for the trial and the protocol with the FDA specified that indi-viduals with "closed epiphyses" were not eligible to participate. When I searched online I found the following definition for closed epiphyses: The epiphyses (i-PIF-uh-sees) are centers of growth, extending from the ends of our long bones. The epiphyses remain open while a person still has potential for growth; when the epiphyses are closed, there is no potential for growth. I wrote to Alex that it looked like I found a loophole because even though Rebecca apparently had little potential for growth, she met the criteria - and time was running out.

That afternoon I finally received a call back from Dr. Imperato, Chief of Adult Endocrinology from New York Presbyterian. She said "Rebecca does indeed meet the criteria according to the protocol, if she has some open growth plates, she does have growth potential, and therefore does not have closed epiphyses."

Like Dr. Vogiatzi, she felt confident that Rebecca could take IGF-1 safely for such a short period of time and that she was still growing. She also said that even if they would not allow Rebecca to participate, in a similar situation for another child who did not meet the criteria for a clinical trial, she had appealed to the National Institutes for Health and made a plea for compassionate use of a different drug and was able to obtain approval with a protocol specifically designed for that child.

She was also very nonchalant about the potential side effects of taking IGF-1 especially because it would not be administered for a very long period of time, and the fact that they were giving her (a 15 year old) the same dose that a 5 year old would take. She said we could closely observe any changes in Rebecca and stop administering the medication if it seemed to be causing any problems.

She too took a great deal of time speaking with me, and then she said "I spoke to Rob and he was not opposed to Rebecca participating in the trial." He told her "if it's okay with the research team it's okay with me". He then told her to ask me to call him. I replied "that's great, but who is Rob" and she said "Rob Rapaport, the endocrinologist." That made no sense at all because this was the same doctor who had been saying no all along. She said he would like me to call him because it was the researchers who were having an issue with Rebecca participating. It was remarkable that Dr. Imperato took it upon herself to call "Rob" on our behalf.

I spoke with Dr. Rapaport the next morning and I was left even more confused. While he said he would not be opposed to Rebecca receiving the growth hormone, he felt her growth plates were essentially closed, despite the fact that five other doctors were confident that she still had growth potential. Although we discussed the fact that she did not have "closed epiphyses" and that with her slight potential for growth meant she would be eligible according to their FDA protocol, he still would not recommend that she take part in the trial.

It was an extremely frustrating call but later that morning Dr. Rapaport seemed to have a change of heart. I heard from Alex who said Dr. Rapaport was willing to consider a compromise. He would look at an X-ray of Rebecca's knee to determine if other growth plates were open enough to give him a greater comfort level. I immediately checked with my cousin Craig to see which growth plates were the last to close and he said to have them look at the clavicle and Alex agreed to look at those growth plates too.

That evening we took Rebecca to Englewood Hospital again for X-rays (8 different views) and unfortunately their computers were down and they were unable to generate the films so we had to wait until the next morning.

We planned on driving into the city to drop them off, and I once again took photos of the X-rays using my iPhone and sent them to my cousins. What an incredible day and age we live in where we have this amazing technology that enabled me to instantaneously communicate with all of the involved parties and transmit images through text messages and email.

My cousin Craig wrote back "the films, while showing a fair bit of closure, also show some open physis. The distal femur (top bone of the knee) looks somewhat closed, while the proximal tibia (bottom bone of the knee) shows a small amount of open physis. The proximal humerus (top part of the arm bone) though reveals a fair amount of unfused physis (which is good). So, it is a mixed bag; that being said, there is enough to argue that not all the bones are fully fused yet...though close."

This was great news. We dropped the X-rays off for Alex. Two hours later, and one excruciatingly painful week after his fateful call telling us the bad news, we heard back from him - Rebecca was back in the trial!

We couldn't believe the news and were so incredibly excited and grateful to everyone who was involved. Alex said we should be able to get started in a few weeks after Rebecca has completed a few more routine tests. When we brought Rebecca for her an echocardiogram which was one of the requirements for medical clearance, Michey asked when we would start with the injections. Alex said "we're going as fast as we can to try to keep up with Jon time but we can only move so fast".

Because we were successful in getting Rebecca back into the program, the next step was a visit to the Rutgers Sensory-Motor Integration Lab in New Jersey. They were breaking new ground by applying the technology used in movies, a $100,000 system, to produce computer-generated imaging (CGI) to measure her gait. They attached 15 sensors to her clothing to capture her movements and compare her walking before and after taking the growth hormones to help detect even the most subtle changes/improvements that might be imperceptible to the naked eye. This would be the first time it would be used with someone with autism. (http://www.youtube.com/watch?v=CaHQa6eiQQg)

Two weeks later on a Friday we went in for the final tests - an EKG and blood work - and on Saturday night we received confirmation that Rebecca was medically cleared to begin the trial. We were very excited to receive the news and were cautiously optimistic, because there was no guarantee that this would help Rebecca. We were very happy to know that Rebecca would be able to participate and have a chance to benefit from this incredible groundbreaking research.

We started the trial shortly thereafter and began to administer shots to Rebecca twice a day. As part of the study, we were told that Rebecca would have either a placebo or the growth hormone for the first 12 weeks, and vice versa after that time — but we wouldn't know whether or not is was the drug or the placebo in each 12 week period. Apparently it has been found that parents observing their children using a placebo, when they don't know it is a placebo, report 30% improvements on average in their children.

I didn't think it was fair to make Rebecca have two shots a day if she wasn't receiving the drug so I starting talking about getting the vials tested to see what they really contained. As you can imagine this didn't go over very well with my family, and everyone was upset that I might jeopardize the study and put Rebecca at risk of getting disqualified again. I told Alex about my intentions and he wasn't very happy about the idea.

A few nights later, before I was scheduled to go out of town to see a friend who owned a pharmaceutical company who could probably test the substance to determine if in fact it was the growth hormone, I took a very small sample from one of the vials and wrapped it carefully in a small red bag surrounded by cushioning that would easily fit in my carryon bag with an ice pack inside to keep it cold. I stashed away this little package in the back of the garage refrigerator.

The next day I went out of town and that night I told Michey to send Sam downstairs to retrieve a special red package from the fridge. Michey was very happy to have found out that I decided for her, for Alex, and for science, to leave things the way they were supposed to be and follow the rules for once in my life.

LESSONS LEARNED
Get the facts
It is more important than ever to make sure you ask for copies of medical re-

cords, X-rays, and find out everything you can about any medical issue involving a family member and to get second (or third) opinions.

We wouldn't give up, especially because the stakes were so high and as a result of the following:

1. Rebecca has an extremely rare disorder and there was some hope that the use of growth hormones might help improve her life in some way.
2. When they interpreted the X-rays and determined that Rebecca's growth plates were closed it meant she would be excluded from the clinical trial.
3. If her growth plates were closed, the use of growth hormones could be dangerous.

The first thing I wanted to know was what side effects Rebecca might experience if we were to somehow obtain the growth hormone on our own. Armed with the knowledge that the risks of side effects were relatively low because of the short duration of the study, I gained greater confidence to proceed.

Use every possible resource

I am fortunate to have some very smart cousins who are doctors and they got involved right away. They gave me great advice and directed me to other doctors who could help. They also encouraged me to question the findings of the researchers because in their opinion Rebecca's growth plates were not completely closed. They in turn put me in touch with other doctors who helped build our case that Rebecca should be able to participate.

Think outside the box

On hearing that Rebecca didn't qualify because she had "Closed Epiphyses", one of the exclusion criteria for the clinical trial, I immediately searched for and found the definition and realized that I had discovered a loophole.

Don't give up

Keep trying because in many situations you have nothing to lose. As my dad has always said when talking about pursuing a sales opportunity "if it doesn't work out you will be no worse off than you would have been otherwise and at least you will know you have given it your all."

###

Get the whole story about Driven on: www.DrivenStory.com
Send comments, questions or suggestions to singer@eimpulse.com

13936061R00065

31901051532564

Made in the USA
Charleston, SC
10 August 2012